The Beatitudes

Living out the Heart of Christ

Prasanth Jonathan

Table of Contents

Dedication

Dedicated to My Lord and Savior, Jesus Christ,

Who gave His life for me, that I might find life in Him.

In His boundless love, I have discovered grace.

In His sacrifice, I have received redemption.

In His teaching, I have found the path to true blessedness.

May this book be a humble offering to the One who is worthy of all honor and praise!

Acknowledgment

I thank my Lord and Savior, Jesus Christ, whose mercy and grace have allowed me the privilege of serving Him for the past 25 years.

I extend my heartfelt gratitude to Pastor Samson Kottoor, Senior Pastor of City Changers in Cochin, Kerala, India, for writing the foreword for this book and for his unwavering encouragement throughout this journey.

I am also deeply thankful to my brothers and sisters at Thompson First Baptist Church, Canada, who took the time to read the manuscript and offered invaluable suggestions to enhance this work.

I want to honor my parents for their sacrifices and for instilling in me the values that have guided my path.

A special acknowledgment goes to my beloved wife, Dr. Michelle Jonathan. Her unwavering support, love, and patience have been my anchor throughout this writing process. Thank you for being my partner in this ministry and for standing by me through every challenge. I am also grateful to our wonderful children, Joanne and Jeremy, who have been a constant source of joy and motivation. Their understanding and encouragement mean the world to me.

In His grace & for His glory.

Prasanth Jonathan
Thompson, MB,
Canada

About the Author

Prasanth Jonathan is a servant of God with over 25 years of ministry experience spanning India, the United Kingdom, and Canada. Currently serving as the Senior Pastor at Thompson First Baptist Church in Manitoba, Canada, Jonathan is dedicated to guiding others in their journey of discipleship and spiritual growth: to Transform - to Conform - to Christlikeness.

Alongside his pastoral work, he is a gifted lyricist and music composer. Jonathan is blessed to share his life and ministry with his wife, Dr Michelle, and their two children, Joanne and Jeremy. His heart for discipleship and commitment to God's calling shine through his life and ministry, encouraging believers to walk as Jesus walked.

Foreword

It is a great joy and honor for me to write the foreword for this book, "The Beatitudes," authored by Prasanth Jonathan. I have had the privilege of knowing Prasanth for 33 years, ever since God brought him into my life as a young believer seeking to grow in his faith. God granted me the opportunity to disciple him in his early Christian journey, and it has been a blessing to watch him grow into the man of God he is today.

Throughout the years, Prasanth and I have stayed closely connected, and our friendship continues to deepen. From the very beginning, I could see his passion for understanding God's truth and living it out. Even today, I am amazed at how God continues to use him to bless and inspire others. As a pastor, teacher, lyricist, music composer and spiritual leader, Prasanth has always been driven by a desire to guide others towards a deeper understanding of God's truth.

This book, "The Beatitude," is a true reflection of Prasanth's heart for discipleship and Christian living. In this book, he brings to life the teachings of Jesus from the Sermon on the Mount, offering a fresh perspective that will serve as an eye-opener to many. His insights are not just theoretical but are grounded in practical, everyday applications that can transform lives and lead believers into a deeper walk with Christ.

I believe this book will be a great blessing to all who read it. May you be transformed, renewed, and empowered as you read these words and take them to heart.

With deep love and prayers,

Samson Kottoor
Founder& Senior Pastor
City Changers Church, Cochin
India

The Beatitudes

1 And seeing the multitudes, He went up on a mountain, and when He was seated His disciples came to Him.

2 Then He opened His mouth and taught them, saying:

3 "Blessed are the poor in spirit, For theirs is the kingdom of heaven.

4 Blessed are those who mourn, For they shall be comforted.

5 Blessed are the meek, For they shall inherit the earth.

6 Blessed are those who hunger and thirst for righteousness, For they shall be filled.

7 Blessed are the merciful, For they shall obtain mercy.

8 Blessed are the pure in heart, For they shall see God.

9 Blessed are the peacemakers, For they shall be called sons of God.

10 Blessed are those who are persecuted for righteousness' sake, For theirs is the kingdom of heaven.

11 Blessed are you when they revile and persecute you, and say all kinds of evil against you falsely for My sake. 12 Rejoice and be exceedingly glad, for great is your reward in heaven, for so they persecuted the prophets who were before you.

Seeking

the Heart of the Master

Understanding the Compassionate Preacher

Imagine being part of the crowd gathered on that mountainside, listening to Jesus, the greatest preacher the world has ever known. What would that have felt like? His words weren't just wise sayings from a teacher—they were divine revelations straight from the heart of God Himself. Jesus wasn't just teaching people how to live better lives; He was speaking as the Son of God, the final Judge, the one who fully understands human nature.

Jesus, who preached the Beatitudes, was more than just a teacher. He was divinely qualified to speak about the subjects He expounded. As the Son of God, He spoke with authority. As a King, He declared the blessings of His kingdom. As a Savior, He showed us the way to true blessedness. The Beatitudes were more than just words of comfort—they were declarations of the character of the citizens of His kingdom.

Jesus, who is the Son of God and our Savior, knew better than anyone what it means to be truly blessed. He didn't just preach these words; He lived them. As the ultimate source of blessing, He was perfectly equipped to tell us who is truly blessed and what it means to be blessed in the eyes of God. Because of this, when Jesus declares who is blessed, it's not just His opinion—it's the truth. This is why we must pay close attention to His words.

It's important to understand that the Beatitudes aren't a list of how to earn salvation. Instead, they describe the characteristics of those who are already experiencing God's grace in their lives. They reveal the heart and life of someone who follows Jesus. As our Good Shepherd, Jesus recognizes His followers, and He alone can accurately identify those who are truly blessed. As the Judge, He would one day separate the blessed from the cursed, and here, in the Beatitudes, He gave us the marks of the truly blessed.

The First Word of Grace

Jesus began with the word "blessed"—not once, but over and over again, He speaks of the blessed life. The word "blessed" is a term that signifies deep joy and fulfillment. According to Strong's Definitions, the Greek word used here, *makários*, means "supremely blest," "fortunate," and "well off"—essentially, it denotes a happiness that transcends earthly conditions. This "blessedness" is not fleeting or circumstantial; rather, it's a joy rooted in our alignment with God and His kingdom.

As we journey through each Beatitude, we find that being "blessed" is inseparably tied to our sanctification. As we grow in humility, mercy, purity, and peace, God grants us this state of blessedness—an enduring joy that every heart desires. This joy isn't an escape from suffering or a guarantee of earthly comfort; rather, it's a joy that sustains us through trials, molds our character, and draws us closer to Christ. Each Beatitude invites us deeper into the life of Christ, offering a blessing that is both present and eternal, fulfilling the human longing for true happiness.

This theme of blessedness is not merely a reward at the journey's end but accompanies us at every stage of our sanctification, uniting them under a promise of joy that is found only in God. Thus, the Beatitudes not only outline a path of sanctification but also affirm that in every step toward Christlikeness, we experience the fullness of God's blessing, drawing us into the joy that so many seek.

From Curse to Blessing

The last word in the Old Testament is "curse" (Malachi 4:6 " And he will turn the hearts of the fathers to the children, And the hearts of the children to their fathers, Lest I come and strike the earth with a *curse)* but the first word in Jesus' sermon is "Blessed," which means a new time of grace and hope. This shift is from condemnation to blessing, from judgment to mercy, from rejection to grace. This compassion continues throughout His teachings and His life, showing us that Jesus' teaching isn't just intellectual; it's deeply relational and compassionate.

The Ladder of the Beatitudes

The Beatitudes are like the steps of a ladder—a step-by-step progression that leads us closer to Christ day by day - each step ascending to a higher level of spiritual experience. Imagine standing at the base of a tall ladder, holding a lantern that casts a soft glow in the darkness. You can only see the first step, but as you place your foot on it, the light reveals the next rung. With each step you take, the lantern illuminates the next step to guide you upward.

However, the journey of sanctification reflected in the Beatitudes is not a simple, linear path where each step must be completed before moving on to the next. Rather, these qualities develop one after the other and grow side by side, each one essential and interconnected as we are gradually transformed into the likeness of Christ.

This is how the journey of the Beatitude works—each step leads you closer to Christ. With every ascent, God unveils the next aspect of spiritual growth. They aren't random statements thrown together but are carefully ordered to reflect the spiritual journey of a disciple. Each beatitude builds upon the one before it, guiding you into a deeper relationship with God, showing that with each step, you become more like Christ and draw closer to Him.

Where Weakness Becomes Strength

The Beatitudes present a series of divine paradoxes—statements that contradict worldly wisdom but reveal deeper spiritual truths. For example, "Blessed are they that mourn, for they shall be comforted." Mourning is usually seen as a negative experience, yet Jesus calls those who mourn blessed. This is not mourning for worldly loss but for our own sin. Meekness is often mistaken for weakness in modern society, but Jesus said, "Blessed are the meek, for they shall inherit the earth" which challenges the aggressive and self-promoting attitudes often celebrated by society.

A Call to Radical Discipleship

Each Beatitude has two parts: the condition (poor, mourn, meek, hunger for righteousness, merciful, pure in heart, peacemakers, persecuted) and the promise (kingdom of heaven, comfort, inheriting the earth, being filled, mercy, seeing God, being called sons of God). Together, they paint a picture of the ideal follower of Christ and the rewards both in this life and in eternity.

Beatitudes start with humility, recognizing our need for God's help—this is the foundation for all spiritual growth. From there, we progress through mourning over sin, meekness, and a hunger for righteousness. Each of these traits reflects more and more of Jesus' character. He lived exactly what he preached. He showed the way and called his disciples to live as he lived.

So, as we study the Beatitudes, we'll see that they describe a journey of transformation—a journey toward becoming more and more like Christ. In these teachings, we see that true blessedness often comes in surprising forms—being "poor in spirit," mourning, showing mercy, and even facing persecution. These may seem like contradictions, but Jesus shows us that in God's kingdom, the humble, the meek, and those who seek righteousness are the ones who truly inherit the earth and find comfort, mercy, and, ultimately, the kingdom of heaven.

The Beatitudes describe the character of those who are part of God's kingdom. They are not prescriptions for how to be saved but descriptions of those who are saved. They reveal the marks of a life transformed by grace. The Beatitudes are more than just comforting promises; they are a radical call to discipleship. They offer a blueprint for a life that is counter-cultural and focused on God's kingdom rather than earthly success. Each Beatitude invites the believer into a deeper relationship with God, encouraging them to trust in His provision and purpose, even when the world stands opposed.

Living in God's Blessings now and forever

By living out the Beatitudes, we demonstrate the character of Jesus to the world. We become the "salt of the earth" and the "light of the world," shining forth God's goodness and preserving His truth in a broken world. As we climb this spiritual ladder—from poverty of spirit to persecution for righteousness' sake—we grow in our identity as children of God and in our capacity to bring His kingdom to earth.

In the end, the Beatitudes are not simply about enduring hardship but about living in the fullness of God's blessing, both now and for eternity.

Blessed are the poor in spirit, for theirs
is the kingdom of heaven.

Chapter 1

"Blessed are the poor in spirit, for theirs is the kingdom of heaven." (Matthew 5:3)

By living out the Beatitudes, we demonstrate the character of Jesus to the world. We become the "salt of the earth" and the "light of the world," shining forth God's goodness and preserving His truth in a broken world. As we climb this spiritual ladder—from poverty of spirit to persecution for righteousness' sake—we grow in our identity as children of God and in our capacity to bring His kingdom to earth.

What Does It Mean to Be Poor in Spirit?

What does it mean to be "poor in spirit"? It's not about being financially poor or emotionally downcast. Jesus is talking about something much deeper, something at the core of who we are. Being poor in spirit is about recognizing our need for God. It's about understanding that no matter what we have in life—whether it's wealth, intelligence, or influence—none of it brings true fulfilment without God. At the heart of this Beatitude is a deep humility, a kind of spiritual poverty where we acknowledge that we can't do life on our own. Think about a ladder. If the first step is too high, no one will be able to climb it. But Jesus starts at the very bottom, right where we are, so everyone can begin their journey.

Imagine standing before God with nothing in your hands to offer—no achievements, no good deeds that could ever measure up.

It's a humbling experience, but it's also freeing. This kind of humility creates space in our hearts for God to fill. When we come to Him with empty hands and open hearts, we are blessed. In fact, Jesus says that the kingdom of heaven belongs to people like this—people who recognize their need for Him and depend on His grace.

The human heart is often ruled by a desire to possess things- more wealth, better status, power and the approval of others, but Jesus calls us to surrender all these desires (Matthew 6:19-20). Jesus addressed this when He said we must deny ourselves, take up our cross, and follow Him (Matthew 16:24, Luke 14:27). True freedom comes when we let go of our attachment to worldly possessions and allow God to reign in our hearts.

Pride: The Root of Spiritual Blindness

What is the one sinful attitude that keeps people from turning to Jesus Christ to be saved?

This sinful attitude can be summed up in one word: pride.

We might define it as "spiritual self-sufficiency." – It is the confident belief that we can stand before God as acceptable based on our own merits or actions. The opposite of "poor in spirit" would be "wealthy in spirit", the concept that we possess within ourselves everything we need or desire. This is the leading philosophy of modern society. It is called 'expressive individualism'. It is the idea that meaning, and identity aren't given to me by somebody (parents, church, or God) but rather are found within me.

Expressive Individualism: The Modern Misconception

The goal of expressive individualism is to discover and express one's inner desires. This worldview is evident in popular slogans such as:

- *You be you.*
- *Be true to yourself.*
- *Believe in yourself.*
- *Live your Truth.*
- *Your happiness is what matters.*

Basically, it is a philosophy of living without genuine reference to God, where the authentic "you" and your feelings about yourself --are your god. Expressive individualism says that authenticity is the most important thing in life and that people should live their lives in line with their deepest desires in order to be authentic.

When the world says You be you, Love yourself - Jesus told His disciples, "If anyone desires to come after Me, let him deny himself, and take up his cross, and follow Me." (Matthew 16:24)

When the world says Follow your heart – Jesus said, "Follow me, "The heart is deceitful above all things, And desperately wicked;" Jeremiah 17:9-10

When the world says Believe in yourself – Jesus said, "Believe in me. "I am the way, the truth, and the life. John 14:6

When the world says Live your Truth – Jesus said, "I am the truth, know the truth, and the truth will set you free." John 8:31-32

When the world says Your happiness is all that matters - Jesus said, "For what will it profit a man if he gains the whole world, and loses his own soul? Or what will a man give in exchange for his soul?" Mark 8:36-37

But it is pride that has been wrapped up in catchy phrases like "be true to yourself." When someone is proud, everything becomes about the three things: I, me, and myself.

The World's View vs. Christ's Perspective

The world around us often sends the opposite message. We're told to be self-sufficient, to pursue success at all costs, and to take pride in our accomplishments. But Jesus flips this on its head. He says that real joy, real happiness, and real blessedness come from acknowledging our spiritual neediness and acknowledging our spiritual nothingness!

The poor, in spirit, are blessed because they have stopped relying on themselves and they started relying on God. It's all about acknowledging that we are spiritually bankrupt on our own. We're like someone stranded in the desert, desperate for water, fully aware that nothing we have can quench our thirst. Think this up: you are in the middle of a desert, with no water in sight. You're desperate, you're thirsty, and you know that you can't survive on your own. That's how we are spiritually without God. To be "poor in spirit" means to realize that we are spiritually empty without Him, being fully aware that we can do nothing on our own to quench our deep spiritual thirst. This can be a hard realization, especially in a world that praises independence and self-made success. We have an attitude to say to the Lord, "Lord, I need You now. I cannot live my life without your guidance, without your grace, and without your strength; give me wisdom to judge my self-help me to look with in me, help me to understand my spiritual poverty". This is the attitude we need to be poor in the spirit.

Jesus teaches us that acknowledging our need for God is the key to entering His kingdom. When we see ourselves as "poor in spirit," we make room for God's grace to fill us. In Isaiah 66:2, God says, "But on this one will I look: on him who is poor and of a contrite spirit, and who trembles at My word." God values a humble heart that comes to Him in need, not one that is full of pride or self-reliance. God gives grace to the humble! Just as a river flows naturally from a high place to a low one, so does God's grace flow toward those who are humble. The higher a person exalts themselves, the less they can receive this life-giving flow. But when we lower ourselves in humility, just like the low valleys receive the full blessing of the river, we open our hearts to receive God's abundant grace. James 4:6 reminds us that "God resists the proud but gives grace to the humble."

In 2 Corinthians 12:9, he writes, "And He said to me, 'My grace is sufficient for you, for My strength is made perfect in weakness.'" Paul understood that it was through his weaknesses that God's strength shined the most. Instead of boasting about his accomplishments, he found joy in relying on God's strength. So, as we look at the world's message of self-sufficiency, we can choose to follow Christ's perspective instead. Jesus calls us to stop trusting on ourselves or on our own strength and to come to Him, with empty hands and in need. Only then can we experience the real blessings of His kingdom. His strength is made perfect in our weakness.

Humility in Action

Jesus' story about the Pharisee and the Tax Collector is a great example of how this attitude is different from the attitude that is talked about in the first Beatitude. Look at the two opposite attitudes:

9Now He also told this parable to some people who trusted in themselves that they were righteous and viewed others with contempt: 10"Two men went up into the temple to pray, one a Pharisee and the other a tax collector. 11The Pharisee stood and began praying this in regard to himself: 'God, I thank You that I am not like other people: swindlers, crooked, adulterers, or even like this tax collector. 12I fast twice a week; I pay tithes of all that I get.' 13But the tax collector, standing some distance away, was even unwilling to raise his eyes toward heaven but was beating his chest, saying, 'God, be merciful to me, the sinner!' 14I tell you, this man went to his house justified rather than the other one; for everyone who exalts himself will be humbled, but the one who humbles himself will be exalted." (Luke 18:9-14).

The Pharisee "trusted in himself" that he was good in God's eyes, which is another word for "spiritual self-sufficiency." He thanked God for making him better than other people by standing tall and proud in front of him. He talked about other men's sins and said that he was not like those men. He was proud of what he did, like fasting twice a week and giving away ten percent of everything he owned. He put himself up. He believed he was "spiritually self-sufficient."

But the poor tax collector was not. He was not even brave enough to "raise his eyes to Heaven" because he didn't feel free to "stand" in front of God. He was too humbled to compare himself to other people because he knew he was a much worse sinner. He couldn't use any good deeds as an excuse because he realized that his sins were so bad that they overshadowed any good he may have done.

In fact, he couldn't do anything else in front of God but hit himself in the chest to show how sorry he was for his sin...all he could do was beg God to forgive him, saying, "Be merciful to me a sinner!"

Jesus says that the Pharisee went home "unjustified," which means that God did not see him as righteous. The Pharisee was still happy with himself, but he was lost in his sins, and God did not see him as righteous. It was the poor, needy, helpless, and pitiful tax collector who went home that day justified. He had no sense of self-sufficiency and could only cry out to God in his sinfulness and beg for mercy.

The Kingdom Belongs to the Broken

When Abraham interceded with the Lord about the fate of Sodom and Gomorrah, he humbly said, " Then Abraham spoke up again: "Now that I have been so bold as to speak to the Lord, though I am nothing but dust and ashes," (Genesis 18:27). Abraham recognized his insignificance and approached God with deep humility.

When God called Moses to lead His people out of Egypt, Moses responded with humility and self-doubt: " But Moses said to God, "Who am I, that I should go to Pharaoh, and that I should bring the sons of Israel out of Egypt? Please, Lord, I have never been eloquent, neither recently nor in time past, nor since You have spoken to Your servant, for I am slow of speech and slow of tongue." (Exodus 3:11; 4:10).

But the LORD said to him, "Who has made the human mouth? Or who makes anyone unable to speak or deaf, or able to see or blind? Is it not I, the LORD? 12Now then go, and I Myself will be with your mouth and instruct you in what you are to say." (Exodus 4:11-12). God's response to Moses was not to boost his self-esteem but to redirect his focus to God's power and presence. James 4:6: "God resists the proud, but gives grace to the humble."

John the Baptist said, "I baptize with water; but among you stands one whom you do not know, even he who comes after me, the thong of whose sandal I am not worthy to, He must increase, I must decrease" (John 1:27; 3:30). Jesus said of John the Baptist, "Among those born of women, none is greater than John" (Luke 7:28). John lived out the principle that "If anyone would be first, he must be last of all and servant of all" (Mark 9:35).

When Jesus was not far off from the house, the centurion sent friends to him, saying to him, "Lord, do not trouble yourself, for I am not worthy to have you come under my roof; therefore, I did not presume to come to you. But say the word, and let my servant be healed" (Luke 7:6-7). Jesus marveled at his faith and said, "I tell you, not even in Israel have I found such faith." (Luke 7:9).

The Apostle Paul openly acknowledged his own unworthiness, saying, "I know that nothing good dwells within me, that is, in my flesh" (Romans 7:18). He also said, "We have this treasure in earthen vessels to show that the transcendent power belongs to God and not to us" (2Corinthians 4:7). He considered himself "the foremost of sinners; " (1 Timothy 1:15-16).

What is Poverty in the Spirit?

Being poor in spirit is

A sense of powerlessness in ourselves.

A sense of nothingness and helplessness before God.

A sense of moral uncleanness before God.

A sense of personal unworthiness before God.

A realization that if there is to be any life or joy or usefulness, it will have to be all of God and all of grace.

Actually speaking, though everyone is, in reality, poor in spirit—no one can truly be spiritually self-sufficient—not everyone recognizes or lives in this truth. But Jesus calls those who acknowledge their spiritual poverty "blessed" because they're open to receiving God's grace."

So, how do we live with this "poor in spirit" attitude? It starts with being honest—with God and with ourselves. We come to God each day and admit we need His grace. We let go of our pride and our need to control everything, and we trust in His goodness. This humility is where true happiness begins.

To live with a "poor in spirit" attitude, we need to start by being honest with ourselves and with God. Each day, we can come to Him and admit our need for His grace. Like David said in Psalm 51:17, "The sacrifices of God are a broken spirit, a broken and contrite heart—these, O God, You will not despise." True happiness and blessing come when we humbly accept our need for God and surrender to His love.

Who is Blessed?

When Jesus says, "Blessed are the poor in spirit," He does not mean everyone. He means those who feel it- who understand it. Blessed - approved by God - are the people who keenly feel their inadequacies, helplessness, unworthiness, and emptiness. They do not hide these things under self-sufficiency but are honest about them, grieved by them, and driven to seek and put total dependence on the grace of God. These people are blessed not because they are perfect but because they are honest with themselves. Think about your own life. Are there any areas where you've been trying to hide your weaknesses or put on a strong front? Maybe it's time to let go of that self-sufficiency and come to God with an honest and open heart- with any mask - just as you are. God blesses those who don't pretend to be perfect and ready to seek His grace.

The Biblical Solution to Feelings of Unworthiness

When a person is broken by a sense of guilt or unworthiness, the solution is not self-esteem. When God called Moses to lead the Israelites out of Egypt, Moses felt completely inadequate. He said, "Who am I that I should go to Pharaoh, and that I should bring the children of Israel out of Egypt?" (Exodus 3:11). Moses saw his weaknesses—he understood he wasn't a good speaker, and he felt unqualified. But God did not tell Moses, "Stop putting yourself down- You are somebody - You are eloquent." No. That is not the biblical way. Instead, God said, "Stop looking at your own unworthiness and stop looking at your uselessness- but look at me- trust in me - put all your confidence in me - I made your mouth. I will be with you. I will help you. I will teach you what to say. Look to me and live!" Shifting the focus from himself to focus on the ability of the sovereign God. God is the One who provides the strength we lack. The biblical answer to low self-esteem is not high self-esteem; it is sovereign grace. Our worth is found in His grace.

Being poor in spirit is not about elevating ourselves or our abilities but about looking to God, trusting in His strength, trusting in His guidance and surrendering to His sovereignty. When we realize that all we have and all we come from God, we begin to live in the freedom of relying on Him instead of ourselves.

The power of Humility

This humility isn't about weakness—it's about finding strength in God. In God's Kingdom, true greatness is found in humility, not in seeking positions of honor, but in submitting to His will. Andrew Murray said, "Humility is the displacement of self by the enthronement of God."

As Paul writes, "He said to me, 'My grace is sufficient for you, for My strength is made perfect in weakness.' Therefore, most gladly I will rather boast in my infirmities, that the power of Christ may rest upon me" (2 Corinthians 12:9). It's in recognizing our weaknesses that we open ourselves to God's strength. Without humility, we cannot admit our weakness, and we cannot open ourselves to God's strength when we stop trying to prove ourselves and start living in the joy of knowing that God's love and grace are sufficient. The Bible tells us, "Humble yourselves in the sight of the Lord, and He will lift you up" (James 4:10). God promises to bless those who humble themselves before Him. As we live with this humble heart, we truly begin to experience the life Jesus offers—a life filled with purpose- a life guided by His love and - a life marked by the presence of the Almighty God.

The Kingdom of Heaven

John the Baptist was the first to talk about this kingdom, calling people to turn away from their sins and prepare their hearts. The central theme of Jesus' preaching was "The Kingdom of Heaven". Jesus began His ministry by proclaiming, "The kingdom of God is at hand. Repent, and believe in the gospel" (Mark 1:15). The "kingdom of heaven" is often used interchangeably with "the kingdom of God" in the New Testament. Jesus taught his disciples about the kingdom of God by using different parables (Matthew 13:1-23, Matthew 13:31-33, Matthew 13:44-46). He asked them to live out the Kingdom's Values. He prepared His disciples to carry on the message of the kingdom. He sent them out to proclaim, "The kingdom of God has come near to you" (Luke 10:9), and He instructed them to prioritize it in their lives by "Seek first the kingdom of God and His righteousness" (Matthew 6:33). For Jesus, the kingdom of God was more than a concept—it was the heart of His message. Through His teachings, parables, miracles, and example, He revealed what it means to live under God's rule, offering hope and a pathway to eternal life with God.

When Jesus speaks of the kingdom, He's not just talking about a place we go after we die but about God's active reign in our lives right now. To belong to this kingdom means we are living under God's authority, where His love, His grace, and His justice guide us. In Luke 17:21, Jesus says, "For indeed, the kingdom of God is within you". This kingdom starts in our hearts, transforming us as we allow God to lead us and guide us. Here, the kingdom refers to God's rule and reign, with Jesus Christ as the King. To be part of this kingdom means to live under His authority and enjoy the blessings of His reign.

When Paul said, "the kingdom of God is not eating and drinking, but righteousness and peace and joy in the Holy Spirit" (Romans 14:17), he was pointing to something far deeper than outward actions—he was describing the inner transformation that happens when God rules over our lives. Believers who are citizens of this heavenly kingdom should possess these heavenly qualities. As followers of Jesus, we are called to live according to the principles of this kingdom, which means embodying the righteousness, peace, and joy that come from the Holy Spirit. Sadly, many believers miss out on this life of blessing because they fail to understand the foundation of God's kingdom: humility and repentance.

Kingdom Culture

When you are in God's Kingdom, you are expected to live the same way that Jesus lived -"He who says he abides in Him ought himself also to walk just as He walked "(1John 2:6). For this, you have to learn from him. Matthew 11:29 says, "Take My yoke upon you and learn from Me". What should we learn from Him? The answer is gentleness and humility (Matthew 11:29). He has given an example for us to follow, how to live in God's kingdom.

Now, what should I do to enter God's kingdom? To enter God's kingdom, the first step is repentance—turning away from sin and self-centered living. Without genuine repentance, faith in Christ becomes superficial and ineffective. Repentance is not just about feeling sorry for sin; it is about a complete change of direction—a turning away from sin and a turning toward God. To turn towards God means to leave behind the pursuit of our self-centered goals. Our desire and prayer should be, "Lord, I want to turn away from everything that displeases You. I desire to face You and seek to please You each and every moment of my life." This shift is described in 1 Thessalonians 1:9 as "turning to God from idols." Anything we place above God— be it money, relationships, positions or personal ambitions—can become an idol, diverting our focus away from Him. When we choose to repent and turn toward Him, we begin a new journey that leads us into His kingdom.

This Kingdom life can't be lived by human effort or strength alone. We need the Holy Spirit to live this way, to experience the joy and peace that only He can bring. Just as the rich young ruler failed to see his own need and was unwilling to follow Christ (Matthew 19:16-22:), we must come to a place of acknowledging our need for God. We must compare ourselves not toothers but to God's perfect standard. When we see our shortcomings in light of God's holiness, we understand our need for mercy. Though it seems paradoxical, the truly blessed are those who humbly acknowledge their spiritual poverty. Through Christ, they inherit the fullness of God's kingdom, enjoying its rich blessings now and forever.

Blessed are those who mourn, For they
shall be comforted.

Chapter 2

"Blessed *are* those who mourn, For they shall be comforted."
(Matthew 5:4)

The Heartbeat of Mourning

The second Beatitude takes us deeper into what it means to follow Christ. The second step of the ladder is "mourning" over the sin - which is built upon the first: acknowledging our spiritual poverty. Until you step firmly onto this step of the ladder, you cannot even see the next. Skipping the first step would be like trying to climb a ladder without securing your footing—you'd stumble. In the same way, without recognizing your need for God, you can't fully have the sorrow that leads to repentance and, ultimately, to God's comfort.

In Matthew 5:4, Jesus says, "Blessed are those who mourn, for they shall be comforted." At first glance, this seems like a contradiction. How can mourning lead to blessing? The answer lies in what Jesus is asking us to mourn over—our sin. It's not simply about being sad; it's about having a broken heart for the ways we have hurt God through our actions, thoughts, and desires. It is not enough to intellectually acknowledge that we are sinners—we must also feel - understand – and be aware of - the weight of our sin and experience genuine contrition.

The Power of Mourning

The word "mourn" in this Beatitude comes from the Greek word *'pentheo'*, which describes the deepest kind of grief. Think of the mourning of a nation after a great tragedy or the sorrow a parent feels at the loss of a child. This is the kind of heartache Jesus is talking about—but it's not grief over personal loss or worldly troubles. It's a deep, gut-wrenching sadness over sin—our shortcomings.

We see examples of this kind of mourning in the Bible. Daniel mourned for three weeks over Israel's sin because he recognized the spiritual distance those sins had created between the people and God. (Daniel 10:1-3). Ezra mourned when he realized that the people of Israel had been unfaithful to God. His sorrow wasn't only about the mistake itself but about the fracture it caused in their relationship with God. (Ezra 10:6). Their sorrow wasn't just emotional; it was a spiritual response to the realization of sin.

David's heartfelt lament illustrates how sin can lead to physical and emotional anguish, highlighting the necessity of acknowledging our wrongs. "When I kept silent about my sin, my body wasted away through my groaning all day long. For day and night Thy hand was heavy upon me; my vitality was drained away as with the fever heat of summer" (Psalm 32:3-4).

As Apostle Paul wrote to the Corinthians, "Now I rejoice, not that you were made sorry, but that your sorrow led to repentance. For you were made sorry in a godly manner, that you might suffer loss from us in nothing" (2 Corinthians 7:9 NJKV). Godly sorrow, unlike worldly sorrow, leads to repentance and, ultimately, to forgiveness.

When we fully grasp and understand our own spiritual poverty, we stop trying to justify ourselves and instead turn to God for comfort. And in that place of humility, we find a comfort that goes beyond a temporary fix—it's a comfort that comes from knowing we are truly forgiven and are truly loved. As Psalm 34:18 reminds us, "The LORD is near to the brokenhearted and saves those who are crushed in spirit." (NASB) A broken heart, or contrite spirit, is seen as essential to genuine repentance.

Jesus shows us that while the world might seek happiness without facing its flaws, true peace and joy come from allowing our hearts to be broken over our sins. This brokenness brings us closer to God and leads to a deeper sense of spiritual healing.

A Heart Check of Genuine Sorrow vs. Worldly Sorrow

The world we live in doesn't encourage us to mourn. In fact, it tells us to do the opposite. We live in a culture that celebrates happiness, laughter, and entertainment. We go to great lengths to avoid sadness. The word "amuse" literally means "to not think." In many ways, our society is built on this principle—distracting ourselves from anything that might make us feel uncomfortable, especially when it comes to sin. People love and are attracted to the Epicurean philosophy, " Eat, drink and be merry, for tomorrow we die."

But Jesus turns this thinking upside down. He says, "Blessed are those who mourn, for they shall be comforted." He's teaching us that we can't experience real joy until we've confronted the reality of our sin. There's no true comfort without first acknowledging the brokenness in our hearts. God's way to happiness begins with us being broken over our sins, and it leads to lasting comfort that the world cannot offer.

In 2 Corinthians 7:10, Paul explains the difference between godly sorrow and worldly sorrow: "For godly sorrow produces repentance leading to salvation, not to be regretted; but the sorrow of the world produces death." The sorrow that Jesus talks about isn't about feeling sorry for ourselves; it's about recognizing our mistakes and turning back to God. Mourning leads to repentance, which opens the door to healing and restoration.

Mourning in the Bible: What It Is—and What It's Not

When Jesus talks about mourning in this Beatitude, He's not referring to the kind of sorrow we feel when we lose a loved one or face personal disappointments. Mourning over a loss or an unmet expectation, while painful, is not the same as mourning over sin.

Lessons from the Past

The Bible gives us examples of mourning that were misplaced. One example is Judas Iscariot. After betraying Jesus for thirty pieces of silver, Judas experienced deep remorse; realizing the serious consequences of his actions - He felt sorry about what he did.

However, this remorse was not genuine repentance. In Matthew 27:3-5, we see him returning the silver to the chief priests and elders, declaring, "I have sinned in that I betrayed innocent blood." Instead of turning to Jesus for forgiveness, he lost hope and ended his life (Matthew 27:3-5). He was deeply remorseful - he mourned, and even he felt sorry about his action. However, he was sorrowful for the consequences of his betrayal, not for the change he desired. His mourning brought death instead of life, showing us that feeling sorry isn't enough if it doesn't lead us back to God.

Another example is King Saul. King Saul's story reveals the tragedy of self-deception and an unwillingness to change. Even when confronted with his mistakes, Saul often acknowledged them outwardly, but his heart didn't undergo a real transformation. He mourned over the consequences of his disobedience but not about his disobedience. He never showed true repentance or humility before God (1 Samuel 15:24, 30). His focus was on his reputation, not true repentance, which kept him from experiencing God's forgiveness. This teaches us an important lesson: mere regret or sorrow for mistakes is not enough. True repentance involves a change of heart - Change of action and a desire to align with God's will, not just sorrow over the outcomes of disobedience. We are reminded that God seeks more than external displays of obedience; He desires inner transformation.

Heroes of Mourning

In contrast, real mourning over sin is like the cry of David in Psalm 51. After realizing the depth of his sin, he opens with a plea: "Have mercy upon me, O God, according to Your lovingkindness; according to the multitude of Your tender mercies, blot out my transgressions." (Psalm 51:1). David doesn't minimize his sin or shift the blame to some other person rather, he owns it fully - he mourned over his sin - he accepted he did wrong. David said, "Against You, You only, have I sinned, and done this evil in Your sight" (Psalm 51:4). He felt the weight of his sin before God and confessed it with a broken heart. The entire Psalm 51 reveals David's deep sorrow and brokenness. He mourns not just because he was caught, but because he understands the depth of his offense against God: "Against You, You only, have I sinned, and done this evil in Your sight." (Psalm 51:4). While David's sorrow is deep, his repentance is filled with hope for restoration. He desires not just forgiveness but renewal. He is praying, "Create in me a clean heart, O God, and renew a steadfast spirit within me." (Psalm 51:10). A heart emptied of pride and self-reliance becomes the perfect vessel for God's grace. David's acknowledgment of his sin and his need for God's mercy shows the humility God requires. This is the type of mourning God is looking for.

Why Should We Mourn?

The mourning Jesus is talking about is a response to the realization that our sins nailed Him to the cross. When we see the cross and understand the great cost of our sins, how can we not be moved to mourn? The pain of knowing that our sin caused Christ's suffering should lead us to grief.

James expresses this well when he says, "Draw near to God, and He will draw near to you. Cleanse your hands, you sinners, and purify your hearts, you double-minded. Lament and mourn and weep! Let your laughter be turned to mourning and your joy to gloom" (James 4:8-9). James urges us to face our sins honestly. Mourning isn't about feeling sorry for ourselves; it's about recognizing our faults and getting closer to God. For all who mourn their sin, David's example calls us to bring our broken hearts before God, trusting that He will renew us.

True Mourning Leads to Repentance

True mourning is not just about feeling bad. It leads us to action. When we mourn our sin, we naturally want to turn from it. Paul writes in 2 Corinthians 7:10, "For godly sorrow produces repentance leading to salvation, not to be regretted; but the sorrow of the world produces death". Godly sorrow moves us toward repentance and, ultimately, toward life.

After denying Jesus three times, Peter experiences deep sorrow. Luke 22:61-62 says, "And the Lord turned and looked at Peter. Then Peter remembered the word of the Lord, how He had said to him, 'Before the rooster crows, you will deny Me three times.' So, Peter went out and wept bitterly." His mourning is followed by genuine repentance, leading him to be a foundational leader in the early church.

In the parable of the Prodigal Son (Luke 15:11-32), the son experiences a moment of deep realization about his wrong choices. Luke 15:17 says, "But when he came to himself, he said, 'How many of my father's hired servants have bread enough and to spare, and I perish with hunger!'" This moment of clarity leads him to return to his father. Here, we can see how true mourning leads to repentance and reconciliation.

True mourning over our sins is an essential part of the Christian Walk. It leads us to acknowledge our need for God's grace and mercy, prompting us to seek repentance and ultimately bringing us closer to Him. The journey from mourning to repentance is not easy, but it is vital for our spiritual growth and transformation.

The Comfort God Promises

The amazing promise of this Beatitude is that those who mourn will be comforted. When we confess our sins and mourn over them, God doesn't leave us in our sorrow. He comforts us. 2 Corinthians 1:5 tells us, "For as the sufferings of Christ abound in us, so our consolation also abounds through Christ." Jesus Himself is our comforter. Think about a child who falls and scrapes their knee. They cry, and their parent quickly comes to hug them tight. This is a simple picture of how God comforts us when we're hurting. He doesn't just notice our pain; He actively brings us comfort.

In the end, this comfort is more than just relief from temporary sorrow—it's the promise of eternal joy in the presence of God. In the book of Revelation, we read that in the new heavens and new earth, "God will wipe away every tear from their eyes; there shall be no more death, nor sorrow, nor crying. There shall be no more pain, for the former things have passed away" (Revelation 21:4). Imagine being in a place where there is no sadness or pain. The joy of being with God forever is something we can hardly imagine. This promise of eternal comfort reminds us that our struggles now are temporary, and there is hope that is much greater. When we mourn our sins and turn to God, we can be sure He will comfort us. Just like the father who welcomes back his son, God is waiting to hug us with love and grace.

How Can We Experience True Mourning?

See God for Who He Is

The first step in true mourning is recognizing God's holiness. In Isaiah 6:5, the prophet Isaiah had a powerful encounter with God. He exclaimed, "Woe is me, for I am undone! Because I am a man of unclean lips, and I dwell in the midst of a people of unclean lips; for my eyes have seen the King, the Lord of hosts!" When Isaiah saw God's glory, he immediately realized how far he had fallen short. Imagine standing before a brilliant, radiant light. The closer you get, the more you realize the imperfections in your own shadow. It's similar when we see God's holiness; it shines a light on our own flaws- shortcomings - and sinfulness. The more we are closer to God, the more we are exposed, so that it will help us to understand our nothingness and poverty of spirit which will lead us to the state of mourning over sin.

Pray for a Soft Heart

Another way to experience true mourning is to pray for a heart that is sensitive to sin. Psalm 51:17 says, "The sacrifices of God are a broken spirit, a broken and contrite heart—these, O God, You will not despise." God values a humble heart more than any external sacrifices we might offer. When we ask God to soften our hearts, we become more aware of the weeds of sin in our lives.

Confess Your Sin Immediately

Don't wait. When God reveals sin in your life, confess it and turn away from it. Confession is essential in experiencing true mourning. When God reveals our sin, we shouldn't hesitate to confess it. Psalm 32:3-5 tells us, "When I kept silent, my bones grew old through my groaning all the day long. For day and night, Your hand was heavy upon me; my vitality was turned into the drought of summer. I acknowledged my sin to You, and my iniquity I have not hidden. I said, 'I will confess my transgressions to the Lord,' and You forgave the iniquity of my sin." Imagine carrying a heavy backpack filled with stones. Each stone represents a sin or burden you haven't confessed. The longer you carry it, the more exhausted you feel. But when you finally take it off and hand it over to God, you feel a sense of relief and lightness. Confession frees us from the weight of our sins and allows us to experience God's forgiveness.

When we see God for who He truly is, pray for a soft heart, and confess our sins immediately, we can experience true mourning. This mourning isn't just about feeling sad; it's about recognizing the impact of our actions and longing for a closer relationship with God.

- Seeing God helps us understand His holiness and our shortcomings.
- Praying for a soft heart makes us more sensitive to sin, allowing us to feel genuine sorrow.
- Confessing our sins brings freedom and healing, reminding us of God's incredible grace.

A Life of True Blessing

Mourning over sin is not easy, but it's necessary for a life of true blessing. As Jesus says, "Blessed are those who mourn, for they shall be comforted." It is through mourning that we experience the deep comfort of God's forgiveness and grace. So, let us embrace the call to mourn over our sins, knowing that God's comfort is greater than anything the world offers.

When was the last time you truly mourned over your sin?

Do you believe that god's comfort is far greater than the temporary happiness the world tries to sell?

What changes can you make in your life to align more closely with this teaching of jesus?

The act of mourning over sin is a continuous journey. When we open our hearts to true mourning, we allow God to transform our sorrow into joy. In summary, the second beatitude teaches us that the path to true blessing begins with sincere mourning from the depth of our hearts. Through this mourning, we experience the depth of God's love and the richness of His forgiveness—both now and in the kingdom to come.

Blessed are the meek, For they shall inherit the earth.

Chapter 3

"Blessed *are* the meek, For they shall inherit the earth."
(Matthew 5:5)

The Beatitudes build on each other, and each one is necessary for the next. The third beatitude cannot come first because it depends on the ones that came before it.

The third beatitude talks about true meekness, which can only happen after someone has realized their nothingness and acknowledged their total dependence on God and is mourning about their Sin. How exactly does the meek inherit the earth?

The beatitude journey begins with poverty of spirit, a deep awareness of our insufficiency and complete dependence on God. Recognizing our spiritual emptiness, we understand that without Him, we are nothing. This leads to mourning, where we grieve over our sinful state and the seriousness of our sins against God, a sorrow that drives us to repentance. This godly sorrow naturally leads to meekness and humility as we submit ourselves fully to God's will, knowing that only through His grace can we find redemption and peace.

Who are the Meek?

As I mentioned, these are people whom God has made poor in spirit, leading them to mourn before Him and find His comfort. Here, we also see that they are meek—humble and gentle in spirit, both before God and toward others.

In the Bible, our fallen nature is compared to that of wild animals. For example, in Jeremiah, people are called a wild donkey and a restless camel. But, the grace of meekness softens our temper or that wildness of our character, making us manageable in God's hands. "… You are a swift she-camel running here and there, a wild donkey accustomed to the desert…." (Jer 2:23-24)

In worldly view, meekness is often misunderstood as weakness or passivity, but in reality, it is a powerful virtue that reflects strength under control. It's essential to clarify that meekness is not synonymous with weakness.

In both Psalm 37 and the Beatitudes, meekness embodies a deep-rooted humility that submits to God's will. While the wicked pursue fleeting pleasures through self-serving means, the meek find their delight in the Lord. Their inheritance is not earned through force but received graciously from God.

Meekness, often described by the Greek word "praus", represents strength under control. The terms refer to horses that are tamed, that is, those that follow commands rather than instinct. William Barclay notes that praus is the word for an animal trained to obey, demonstrating that true meekness is about surrendering our power to God's authority. Consider a powerful stallion, strong and wild, galloping across an open field. When tamed by a skilled trainer, the horse learns to follow commands rather than acting solely on instinct. It retains its strength but exercises control, demonstrating that true meekness, like the horse, is strength under control, surrendering our desires to God's authority.   As Christians, this means surrendering our desires and wills to God and letting Him guide our actions.

The Meek are Submissive to God's Will

A meek person doesn't wrestle with God's plans. He trusts that God's will is always good, even when life is difficult. Whether he is placed in times of ease or hardship, he will rest in knowing God's presence is his strength.

Imagine a potter at work, shaping a lump of clay on the wheel. As the potter gently molds the clay, it might feel pressure and discomfort, but it doesn't resist. Instead, it submits to the potter's skilled hands, trusting that he knows what he's doing.

In the same way, a meek person trusts God, the Master Potter, with their life. Whether they're experiencing joy or facing trials, they remain pliable in His hands, believing that God's plans are good. Like Job, who said, "Though He slays me, yet will I trust Him" (Job 13:15), they understand that God's will is supreme. This may be their attitude, "What pleases You, Lord, pleases me."

So, the truly meek are, first of all, submissive to God's will. Whatever God wills, they will.   God's will = My will. What pleases God pleases me! They accept their circumstances, understanding that God's will is supreme. Spurgeon describes it well; "whether God places them in Solomon's palace or Job's trials, they stay content and trusting."

The Meek are Submissive to God's Word

The truly meek is also submissive to God's Word; if he is really meek, he is always willing to submit and surrender to the word of God. He approaches Scripture with an open heart, not trying to mold it to fit their views but instead letting it shape him. Meek do not imagine what the truth should be and then search the Bible for texts to support their 'views; rather, they approach the Scriptures with an open mind, praying, "Open my eyes that I may see wonderful things in your law." (Ps 119:18)

When they encounter doctrines that are hard for flesh and blood to receive, they submit to the Holy Spirit, asking, " Teach me what I do not see; If I have done wrong, I will not do it again' (Job 34:32)" They strive to obey God's instructions out of love, not compulsion. They will "But be doers of the word, and not hearers only" (James 1:22).

The Meek Submits to God's People

Meekness involves submitting to one another out of reverence for Christ. Ephesians 5:21 says, "subject yourselves to one another in the fear of Christ". This submission is cultivated in committed relationships within the church. When we are angry or upset but choose to obey God in the middle of it, we are meek.

The Marks of the Meek

The Meek are Humble

Meekness and humility are closely related yet distinct. Humility is an inward attitude that recognizes our limitations, our need for God, and the importance of others. It is grounded in understanding that we are not self-sufficient and that all we have is by God's grace. Meekness, on the other hand, is how humility is expressed outwardly, particularly in our interactions with others.

A meek man does not consider himself superior to others but knows that he is merely a man and is grateful for the grace of God. He does not boast of his high birth, wealth, or talents. He remembers that he is dust and will return to dust.

If God grants him a lot of grace and makes him useful in his service, he feels more responsible and brings himself down even more in the eyes of God and people. A man with a meek spirit always acts and talks in a humble way, and he does not show the kind of pride that wants others to notice and respect him. A humble heart agrees that everything we are and everything we have is a gift from God. Humility roots us in our dependence on God, while meekness guides our actions toward others with kindness and patience.

C S Lewis said, "Humility is not thinking less of yourself; it is thinking of yourself less". Matthew Henry describes humility as a kind of self-control. True, biblical humility is a self-control of strength that makes us lambs and lions according to the will of God.

True humility is seeing ourselves as we truly are, fallen in sin and helpless and hopeless without God. It is the understanding of our nothingness without God. Jesus' earthly life is the ultimate model of meekness and humility. Though He was the Son of God, He took on human form, embracing life as a humble servant (Philippians 2:6-8). His meekness was strength under control; He had all power but chose restraint, compassion, and gentleness. Jesus described Himself as "gentle and lowly in heart" (Matthew 11:29), inviting us to adopt the same disposition.

The Meek are Gentle

Out of this humility grows gentleness of spirit. The meek man is gentle; he does not speak harshly, his tones are not arrogant, and his spirit is not bossy. He seeks to be a true brother among his brethren, honored to perform even the humblest service for the household of faith.

He is approachable and compassionate, unlike those who repel others with their harshness and pride.

The Meek are Patient

The meek are not only humble and gentle but also patient; they choose not to get easily offended. When others wrong them, they tolerate it and forgive repeatedly, not just once or twice. A meek person might get momentarily angry, as anyone would, but they focus their anger on the wrong action, not the person. This helps them to be as kind to the wrongdoer as if nothing happened.

Christians should work to control their temper and not take offense at small things. Even if someone is naturally quick-tempered, they should seek help from God to manage their anger and not use it as an excuse.

The Meek are Forgiving

In this world, people will sometimes hurt us or try to take away our rights. The meek go beyond just putting up with these wrongs— they freely forgive those who hurt them. Jesus taught us to pray, "Forgive us our debts, as we forgive our debtors," meaning that God forgives us as we forgive others. Holding onto anger or grudges can block our own forgiveness.

This attitude is like Jesus, who prayed for those who crucified him, saying, "Father, forgive them, for they know not what they do." True meekness means letting go of revenge and instead responding to evil with good, following Jesus' example of boundless forgiveness.

The Meek are Content

Finally, meekness involves contentment. The meek-spirited man is not ambitious for worldly gain; he is satisfied with what God provides. His motto is, "God's providence is my inheritance." Whether in abundance or in want, he remains content, trusting that his times are in God's hands. He seeks to use his God-given talents for good but is free from unrest and anxiety, expressing a spirit of thankfulness and peace.

Meekness in Everyday Life

In practical terms, meekness is evident when dealing with difficult people and situations. Imagine having a neighbor who is always bossy and thinks he knows everything. He often criticizes others loudly and insists everyone should follow his rules for the neighborhood. He complains about small things, like the height of someone's grass or how someone is parking their car, and does it in a rude way.

This neighbor is clearly unhappy inside. We can see his frustration and anger in every interaction. At community meetings, He always causes tension by dominating the discussion, interrupting others, and dismissing different opinions. This behavior makes everyone uncomfortable, leading to a lack of harmony in the neighborhood.

Now, imagine if this neighbor learned to be meek. If he learns meekness, his temper will change, bringing peace to himself and those around him. Instead of insisting on his own way, He will start listening to others. He will approach issues with a spirit of cooperation rather than confrontation. He will speak more calmly, show patience, and will be willing to compromise.

Like a horse that has never been tamed, we naturally push God's hand away. But once it is tamed, it is calm and controlled. And as long as we fight God, we will always have problems inside that affect other people.

The Blessing of Meekness

Without meekness, we fall into inner conflict, which comes out as anger, frustration, and turmoil. Meekness brings peace by calming and submitting. Meekness liberates us from pride, rudeness, anger, vengeance, and selfish ambition. Jesus calls us to grow in meekness, gaining control over anger, moderating our passions, and finding contentment and peace in Him.

Meekness in Action

Meekness when opposed

Moses was described as very meek; "Now the man Moses was very humble, more than all men who were on the face of the earth." (Numbers 12:3). He faced a lot of pressure and opposition from the people he was leading. Instead of fighting back against those who complained and spoke against him, Moses chose to pray for them. This shows his meekness and how much he relied on God's strength and guidance.

Moses didn't start out as the meekest man. Early in his life, he struggled with anger. But, over time, God worked in Moses' heart, changing him and teaching him to rely on God's strength and guidance instead of his own anger.

Meekness when provoked

David is another great example of meekness. When Shimei, a man who belonged to the house of Saul, cursed and threw stones at him,

David chose not to fight back (2 Samuel 16:5-14). Instead of getting angry or violent, David accepted the insults and thought that maybe God allowed it for a reason. David could have easily gotten rid of Shimei. But he chose to put up with it- That is meekness.

Meekness When Disappointed

Another example of meekness in the Bible is Apostle Paul. He showed meekness in action when he was deeply disappointed. When he was on trial and expected support from his fellow believers, no one stood by him (2 Timothy 4:16). Paul did not respond with anger or bitterness.

Instead, he prayed for those who let him down, asking that they would be forgiven. He trusted in God's justice and mercy. Paul chose to forgive them.

Meekness When Injured

Jesus showed the ultimate meekness when He was injured and mocked. During His crucifixion, even though He suffered a lot, Jesus did not fight back or make threats. Instead, He entrusted Himself to God (1 Peter 2:23).

Jesus' prayer on the cross, "Father, forgive them; for they know not what they do" (Luke 23:34). It shows His deep forgiveness and love. Even when facing severe injustice and pain, Jesus chose to Love and forgive.

Meekness brings peace and order to our souls by aligning our wills with God's will. It frees us from pride, harshness, anger, vengeance, and ambition by showing itself in humility, gentleness, patience, forgiveness, and contentment. In a believer's life, this is what God's grace does: it makes them more like Christ, who was perfectly meek.

As we grow in meekness, we receive the blessing that Jesus promised: we will inherit the earth.

Blessed are those who hunger and thirst for righteousness, For they shall be filled.

Chapter 4

**"Blessed are those who hunger and thirst for righteousness,
For they shall be filled." (Matthew 5:6)**

As I mentioned before, each of the Beatitudes builds on the one before it. Thus, hungering and thirsting for righteousness is a higher calling. It is the next step after being poor in spirit, mourning and being meek. The first three Beatitudes show us our deep need for God.

We are "poor in spirit" because we realize we can't live the way God wants us to on our own.

We "mourn" because we see how much we have sinned and

We become "meek" because we understand we can't live our lives wisely without God.

Beatitudes are not just a list of virtues but a progression of spiritual truths that describe discipleship. Jesus' teaching in the Beatitudes highlights what it means to live as part of His kingdom. Those who follow Christ have these qualities. In this Beatitude, Jesus introduces a paradox: those who hunger and thirst for righteousness are blessed. We are blessed in our longing because it propels us toward God. As we pursue Him - seek him - we find that our longing is not in vain, for He promises to satisfy those who seek Him earnestly. Psalmist says, "He satisfies the longing soul and fills the hungry soul with goodness" (Psalm 107:9).

When someone stops hungering and thirsting for the things of this world, he becomes ready to seek something better and eternal. We must first lose our passion for earthly pursuits before we can truly desire heavenly ones. "No man can serve two masters;" When selfishness is removed, we become humble and meek, and we will start to hunger and thirst for 'righteousness'.

Before sin entered the world, people lived in perfect happiness and peace because they were perfectly righteous. Just as it was in the Garden of Eden, true happiness in the future will also depend on righteousness. This means that living a truly blessed life is impossible without being right with God. Righteousness—being in a good relationship with God, others, and ourselves—brings a joy that nothing else can replace.

Hunger and Thirst

Hunger and Thirst is a symbol of Need

When you're hungry, your body is telling you it needs food. Similarly, when we hunger for righteousness, it means we recognize we don't have it. It shows the realization and acknowledgement of our sinful condition. Just as we need food and water to survive, our souls crave righteousness. King David said " "O God, You are my God; early will I seek You; my soul thirsts for You; my flesh longs for You in a dry and thirsty land where there is no water." (Psalm 63:1). A person who truly seeks God won't rest until they are in a right relationship with Him and living in a way that pleases Him. This desire for righteousness doesn't fade over time or get satisfied by temporary pleasures. No amount of entertainment or success can fill this need. Just like a hungry person can't ignore their stomach, a believer's soul will keep yearning for righteousness, urging them to find true satisfaction in God. Jesus declares that He alone can satisfy our deepest spiritual hunger and thirst. "And Jesus said to them, I am the bread of life. He who comes to Me shall never hunger, and he who believes in Me shall never thirst." (John 6:35)

Hunger and Thirst is a symbol of Life

Just like a newborn baby naturally cries out for milk, a true Christian naturally hungers for righteousness. This desire is a symbol of Life in us. A spiritually dead person never hungers and thirsts for righteousness.

Hunger and Thirst is a symbol of Health

A healthy person has a good appetite. If we're spiritually healthy, we'll have a strong desire to grow in righteousness. We'll never feel like we've fully arrived, but we will always want more of God's presence and character in our lives.

Hunger and Thirst – A Deep Desire

When Jesus says about those who hunger and thirst, He's talking about a deep, intense desire. Imagine being so hungry or thirsty that you can't think of anything else but food or water. So, hunger and thirst for something is more than just a passing interest; it's a driving force that shapes the choices in our lives.

A Continuous Desire for 'Righteousness'

The verse says that a blessed person desires righteousness above everything else. This longing begins when the Holy Spirit awakens us, making us aware of our sins, our shortcomings, and our unrighteousness before God. We recognize our need for forgiveness and righteousness, asking, "How can I be made right with God?"

Seeking Sanctification

But this hunger for righteousness does not stop there. The blessed still longs for more and more. They not only want to be justified but also long to be transformed.

- The blessed desire a change from inside….
- They desire that their love for sin would change into a love for goodness and holiness.

The hunger and thirst for God and the passion to pursue his righteousness is a hallmark of a true Christian. David says, "As deer pants for flowing streams, so pants my soul for you, O God. My soul thirsts for God, for the living God." Psalm 42:1-2 "O God, you are my God; earnestly I seek you; my soul thirsts for you; my flesh faints for you, as in a dry and weary land where there is no water." Psalm 63:1 The Apostle Paul, even after years of serving Christ, said, "I want to know Him and the power of His resurrection" (Philippians 3:10).

The blessed doesn't stop at justification and regeneration; they also crave sanctification. They pray for God's help to remain pure and truthful, both inwardly and outwardly. They want their character to reflect righteousness, ensuring their actions and words are just and honest.

Longing for Perseverance and Perfection

The blessed continuously seeks to grow in grace and overcome all sinful habits. They pray for perseverance, desiring to become more like Christ each day. Their ultimate goal is to be transformed into Christlikeness.

The more we long for righteousness, the more we experience God's presence and righteousness, the more we experience it…. the more we want it. It's a beautiful cycle of growing closer and closer to God.

What are we Hungering for?

What is our Passion in life?

All of us are looking for satisfaction in life.

What do you think will make you satisfied in life?

What do you think will make you truly happy?

Whatever you believe will satisfy you will become the focus of your life. If you think success will make you happy, then achieving success will become your life's main goal. If you think happiness comes from leisure or retirement, then that will become your life's main focus.

Think for a minute.

What do you think will give you real satisfaction?

Is it being loved?

Is it being appreciated?

Is it getting revenge?

Is it achieving a certain goal or obtaining a specific position?

Whatever you believe will satisfy you.... will become your life's main passion.

Jesus tells us one desire that will truly be satisfied: "Blessed are those who hunger and thirst for righteousness." Why? Because they will be satisfied.

Is this what Christians today are looking for?

Is this what we want from God, or are we after something else?

But what about righteousness?

Do we know what it means to really want this?

We all want to be blessed, but Jesus doesn't say we are righteous if we desire blessings.... He says we are blessed if we desire righteousness.

Let me ask a question-

"Why did Jesus die?"

You may give many answers that are true to the Bible

- He died for our forgiveness

- He died to give us eternal life.

Let us look at some of the key Bible verses about why Christ died.

2 Corinthians 5:15: "He died for all, that those who live should live no longer for themselves, but for Him who died for them and rose again." (2 Corinthians 5:15)

1 Peter 2:24 He "…Himself bore our sins in His own body on the tree, that we, having died to sins, might live for righteousness…" (1 Peter 2:24)

2 Corinthians 5:21: "For He made Him who knew no sin to be sin for us, that we might become the righteousness of God in Him."

The purpose of Jesus' death is that we should desire righteousness. Christ died to save people who no longer live for themselves but who live with a passion for holiness… a passion for righteousness…. a passion for Godliness.

"Blessed are those who hunger and thirst after righteousness, for they will be satisfied."

What do you know about this strong desire for God?

Is this passion growing in you, or is it fading away?

Jesus tells us that those who hunger and thirst for righteousness are blessed because they will be satisfied. This means that if we make righteousness our main pursuit... our passion.... our focus, and our desire..., God promises to fulfill that hunger and thirst.

How can we grow hunger for righteousness?

We can, and we should work on our desire. Paul told Timothy, "Train yourself for godliness" (1 Timothy 4:7). Paul is saying.... "Timothy, there are some things you can do, that will help you grow in godliness.

Think of a young person who spends a lot of time playing video games. He really enjoys these games. He talks about them, thinks about them, plays them, and buys them. He will play games for at least 20 hours a week, and he continues to desire more.

What appetites are shaping our lives?

What is the diet that shaped them?

You like to work out?

You like to sleep?

You like to watch sports?

Read?

Watch lots of movies?

There's nothing wrong with any of these. But ...

Are these holding us back from becoming all that Christ calls us to be?

Is our desire for God being diminished by our hunger and thirst for other things?

The best way to control any craving is to develop a stronger craving for something better. So, how can we develop a desire for holiness? How can we have a greater craving for God and righteousness? If we switch to a healthier diet, it might taste tasteless at first, but over time, we start feeling better. Eventually, our cravings change completely after sticking to the new diet for a while. Similarly

Feed yourself regularly with the Word of God, and after some time, you will have a great hunger and thirst for God.

Feed a congregation the Word of God, and after some time, there will be a church with a great hunger and thirst for God.

Choose to desire Righteousness

Imagine your habits have made you crave TV or video games, and now these habits are holding you back from having a hunger and thirst for God. These activities are not sinful, but the question is

What is your greatest passion?

Where is your heart?

Try taking a break from TV or computer games for a month, or from golf, or from buying new clothes for six months, or from leisure travel. Drop a sport or your hobby for some time. You'll be surprised at the freedom it brings you.

Wean yourself off from the unwanted appetites that are shaping your life.

Trust Christ for Your Growth

"Now may the God of peace Himself sanctify you completely; and may your whole spirit, soul, and body be preserved blameless at the coming of our Lord Jesus Christ. 24He who calls you is faithful, who also will do it." (1 Thessalonians 5:23-24)

Some Christians trust Christ for forgiveness and getting into heaven but feel hopeless about becoming more Christ-like.

They trust Him for justification and glorification but not for sanctification. Yet Christ came to save us from our sins and free us for a better life. He overcame death and hell, sits at God's right hand with all power, and His Spirit lives in you. Christ is your righteousness, sanctification, and redemption (1 Corinthians 1:30).

If you trust Jesus for forgiveness and heaven, you can trust Him to help you grow in righteousness.

Today, check yourself.

Do you have a hunger and thirst for righteousness?

If so, is this passion growing in you, or is it fading away?

Sometimes, you may feel that this chapter is sharp, difficult or hard. We see this in John 6:60, where Jesus preached, "When many of his disciples heard it, they said, 'This is a hard saying; who can listen to it?'"

Today, if you feel any hunger for righteousness, it is Christ who is stirring that in you. He does not do this to mock you. He does this so that you can receive it. He creates this hunger and thirst in you so that you can be satisfied for all eternity.

Blessed are the merciful, For they shall obtain mercy.

Chapter 5

"Blessed *are* the merciful, For they shall obtain mercy."
(Matthew 5:6)

The first four Beatitudes focus on our relationship with God—our hearts, our humility, and our need for Him. The last four Beatitudes shift to how we treat others, reflecting the changes within us. They show us the fruit of our relationship with God.

In the fifth Beatitude, Jesus invites us to show a different kind of mercy. This isn't just about tolerating others or being fair; it's about actively showing kindness and generosity to those around us. This kind of mercy doesn't come naturally to us; it's a gift from God, produced by the Holy Spirit working in us. Through this divine mercy, God changes not only our actions but also our hearts, helping us to be more like Him in how we love and care for others.

Many people think of mercy as simply forgiving someone for their mistakes. While forgiveness is a part of mercy, it is much more than that. Mercy involves compassion and action. John MacArthur, a well-known theologian, explains that mercy comes from a place of love. God is merciful because He loves us deeply. Ephesians 2:4 says, "But God, being rich in mercy, because of His great love with which He loved us." Mercy flows from love and results in forgiveness, but it also goes beyond that.

Here, Mercy is not merely a passive feeling of sympathy; it is an active expression of kindness and generosity towards others, particularly the needy. Spurgeon emphasizes that the blessed ones are not merciful because of inherent qualities or social status but because they have been profoundly impacted by God's grace. They have experienced spiritual poverty, mourned over their sins, and found comfort in God's forgiveness. This transformation enables them to see others through the lens of Christ's love, fostering a deep compassion that prompts them to act.

British Theologian John Stott defines it simply as compassion for people in need. A.W. Pink describes mercy as "a holy compassion of soul, whereby one is moved to pity and go to the relief of another in misery." The Puritan preacher Thomas Watson wrote that mercy is "a melting disposition whereby we lay to heart the miseries of others and are ready on all occasions to be instrumental for their good." Mercy involves the heart, mind, and will. When we see someone in distress, true mercy leads us to feel for them, reflect on their situation, and take action to relieve their suffering. Charles Spurgeon emphasizes that true mercifulness begins with the acknowledgment of our own imperfections.

Mercy involves the heart, mind, and will. True mercy softens our hearts rather than hardening them in response to others' needs. It compels us to think deeply about the suffering of others and consider how we might help. True mercy drives us to be "ready on all occasions to be an instrument for their good."

When we see someone in distress, true mercy leads us to feel for them, reflect on their situation, and take action to relieve their suffering.

Where does mercy come from?

To answer this question, we need to consider the context of the Beatitudes in Matthew 5:3-6, where the first three Beatitudes emphasize the blessing that comes from recognizing our spiritual need: poverty of spirit (verse 3) involves acknowledging our need for God, mourning over our sin (verse 4) means feeling sorrow for the wrongs we've done, and meekness (verse 5) is about accepting life's challenges with humility. When we understand our need and desire God's righteousness, we become open to both receiving and giving mercy. This is like climbing a ladder - one step to another - it is a progression of discipleship.

The progression here is crucial: Mercy flows from a heart that recognizes its own spiritual poverty. When we become aware of our need for God's grace, we are moved to extend that same grace to others. In this sense, "mercy comes from mercy." Our capacity for mercy is rooted in our recognition of God's immeasurable mercy toward us. When we recognize how much we have been forgiven, how deeply we have been loved, and how graciously we have been cared for by God, we become more inclined to extend that same grace to others.

Human Mercy Vs Divine Mercy

The Source of our Mercy

This merciful character grows out of what had already been done for us by the Spirit of God. It is not due to anything in us or our natural character. It is a gift of grace, a fruit growing from the grace we have already received.

The first beatitude already said that "ours is the kingdom of heaven." The second one promised, "We shall be comforted." So, we have already received the mercy of God in the earlier steps.

Thus, we have already obtained mercy, and the fact that we show mercy to others is the result of what God has done for us and in us through the Holy Spirit.

We are merciful not because we are naturally tender-hearted but because we are poor in spirit.

We are merciful not because we had generous ancestors but because we have mourned and have been comforted.

We are merciful not because we seek the approval of others but because we are meek and gentle, inheriting the earth, and wish others could also enjoy the blessings of heaven.

We are joyfully merciful, for we had hungered and thirsted after righteousness, and we had been filled.

When we seek righteousness, God satisfies our hunger and thirst. This fulfilment brings great joy, and this joy overflows into mercy towards others. It is not a burden but a joyful response to the grace we have received. When we understand how much we have been forgiven and blessed, we extend that mercy to those around us.

We are merciful not out of compulsion but out of the freedom and blessing we have received from God.

The Nature of Divine Mercy

This mercy is more than human compassion. It's a reflection of God's own mercy towards us. Human compassion might lead us to feel sorry for others or help them out of duty, but divine mercy goes deeper. It transforms our hearts

- to genuinely care for others,
- to seek their good and
- to act out of love and grace.

Why Mercy Matters?

God is Merciful

Mercy is a fundamental feature of God's character. The Bible describes God as merciful and gracious, slow to anger, and abounding in steadfast love (Exodus 34:6). In Ephesians 2:4-5, it says that God is "rich in mercy," showing us this through His love, which made us alive in Christ. But mercy isn't just something God has; it's a quality He wants us to develop, too. In Hosea 6:6, God tells us, "I desire mercy, not sacrifice, and the knowledge of God more than burnt offerings." This means that God values kindness and understanding more than ritual acts. In Micah 6:8, He calls His people to act justly, love mercy, and walk humbly with Him. Jesus also teaches us to be merciful, just as our Heavenly Father is merciful (Luke 6:36), highlighting mercy as one of the most important values in following God's ways (Matthew 23:23).

God's mercy is forever. David said, "Surely goodness and mercy will follow me all the days of my life" (Psalm 23:6). It is because of God's mercy that we are saved: "He saved us... according to his own mercy" (Titus 3:5). When Paul describes his salvation, he simply says: Even though I was the first among sinners, yet "I received mercy" (1 Timothy 1:13).

Jesus is our Merciful High Priest

Jesus Christ is the perfect representation of God's divine mercy. His ministry was marked by compassion for the marginalized, healing for the afflicted, and grace for the sinner. Through His teachings and life, He demonstrated what it means to be merciful.

Jesus showed mercy in many ways. Consider His mercy to Peter, who denied Him three times. Despite this failure, Jesus prayed for Peter and restored him, showing that mercy means failure does not have the last word (Luke 22:31-32, John 21:17).

The woman caught in adultery (John 8:1-11) is met with mercy instead of condemnation. Jesus does not excuse her sin, but He offers her a second chance. He said, "Neither do I condemn you; go and sin no more." (John 8:11)

In Jesus Christ, God says to His people, "I will be merciful toward their iniquities, and I will remember their sins no more" (Hebrews 8:12).

Jesus is our merciful High Priest. He understands our struggles and invites us to come to Him for mercy and grace in our time of need: "Let us then with confidence draw near to the throne of grace, that we may receive mercy and find grace to help in time of need" (Hebrews 4:16).

We are called to be Merciful

We are called to reflect Jesus' character in our lives. This means being merciful as He is.

Micah 6:8 sums it up: "What does the Lord require of you? To act justly and to love mercy and to walk humbly with your God."

Jesus emphasized mercy over mere ritual sacrifice. Quoting from Hosea 6:6, He says: "I desire mercy, and not sacrifice" (Matthew 9:13).

The Good Samaritan: A Story of Mercy

To understand mercy, let's look into the story of the Good Samaritan. A man is attacked, robbed, beaten, and left for dead. Two travelers see him but pass by without helping. Finally, a Samaritan sees the man, feels compassion, and takes action to help him, bandaging his wounds and ensuring his care.

Jesus asks, "Which of these three proved to be a neighbour to the man who fell among the robbers?" Luke 10:37 gives us the answer, "The one who showed him mercy" (Luke 10:37).

In this story, we see that mercy has two parts:

- Internal: Tenderness of heart -The Samaritan had compassion.
- External: Action - The Samaritan went to him and bound up his wounds.

Living Out Divine Mercy

So, how do we live out this divine mercy in our daily lives?

The Samaritan saw the suffering (verse 33): "A Samaritan, as he journeyed, came to where he was; and he saw him."

A famous quote says, "Eyes that look are common, but eyes that see are rare."

Are we able to see the suffering of those around us? What can we do to make sure we don't neglect people who need help?

The Samaritan had a Caring Compassion (verse 33): "When he saw him, he had compassion. He went to him and bound up his wounds, pouring oil and wine; then he set him on his own beast and brought him to an inn and took care of him."

Do we have a Caring Compassion for those who are suffering? Are we considering it as somebody else's responsibility? When we see someone in need, how do we typically respond? How can we cultivate a heart of compassion that moves us to take concrete actions to alleviate their suffering?

The Samaritan showed Mercy Beyond Boundaries (verse 33): it says, "But a Samaritan…". Despite cultural and religious enmity, the Samaritan helped a Jew who hated him.

Do you find it hard to be kind to certain people or groups because of cultural, social, or personal differences? How can we overcome these barriers to extend mercy and compassion to anyone in need, just as the Samaritan did?

It starts with recognizing our own need for God's mercy. When we see how much we have been forgiven and loved by God, it becomes easier to show that same mercy to others. It means being patient with others, forgiving those who wrong us, and going out of our way to help those in need.

In Matthew 9:13, Jesus said, "Go and learn what this means: 'I want mercy, not sacrifice.'" In the story of the Samaritan, Jesus says, "Go and show mercy like the Samaritan." What does the word 'sacrifice' mean here? - empty religious actions.

It is a warning to all of us that too many people get caught up in religious activities without having an eye to see the suffering of those around them, without feeling compassion, and without making an effort to help.

The Promise of Mercy

Jesus promises that those who are merciful will obtain mercy. This doesn't mean we earn God's mercy by being merciful, but rather, as we show mercy, we continue to receive God's mercy in our lives. It's a lovely cycle of receiving and giving, of grace transforming us and flowing through us to others.

Practical Ways to Show Mercy

Let's consider some practical ways to live out this divine mercy...

- Be quick to forgive those who wrong you. Holding onto grudges only harms us. Forgive as God has forgiven you.
- Look for opportunities to give to those in need. Whether it's time, money, or a listening ear, be generous in your kindness. Let us not be tight-fisted…. open your hands.
- Show empathy towards others. Try to understand their struggles and offer support without judgment.
- Be patient with others' shortcomings. Remember, we all are a work in progress, and everyone deserves grace.

The Impact of Mercy

Living a life of mercy has a great impact not just on those around us but on our own hearts as well.

- It softens our hearts,
- keeps us humble and
- continually reminds us of the grace we have received.

When we are merciful, we become living testimonies of God's love, drawing others to the source of all mercy.

Blessed are the pure in heart, For they shall see God.

Chapter 6

**"Blessed *are* the pure in heart, For they shall see God."
(Matthew 5:8)**

Many teachers focus on changing outward actions, But Jesus aimed at changing our hearts. He knew that the source of all evil lies within and wanted to cleanse it so that our thoughts, words, and actions would be pure. In the Old Testament, we read that "man looks at the outward appearance, but the Lord looks at the heart" (1 Samuel 16:7). Jesus knew this truth well, and His teachings reflected it. He didn't say, "Blessed are those with pure words" or "pure actions"—instead, He blessed those with pure hearts.

Jesus started by blessing the "poor in spirit," showing His concern for our inner nature. He continues with, "Blessed are the pure in heart," highlighting that true purity comes from inside. It's not just about having clean language, actions, or rituals. But more than that… a heart that is clean and in tune with God's will.

Jesus taught that we must be "born again," meaning our inner selves must be renewed by God. Purity of our actions are not enough, but our motives should be pure as well. People may look at our outward behavior, but God looks at our hearts. An impure heart blinds us to spiritual truths. Just as a person with impaired vision can't see clearly, sin distorts our spiritual perception. When our hearts are entangled with sin, like pride, greed, or lust, we can't fully grasp God's goodness, beauty, or holiness.

What is Pure in Heart?

Jesus says the pure in heart are blessed. Since we are sinners and continue to sin, how can we be pure in heart? Purity of the heart means being made clean through the Spirit and the Word of God. We must put God first in every thought, word, and action.

- Staying in God's Word,
- acknowledging our sins,
- repenting when we sin, and
- asking for His forgiveness will guide us to a pure heart.

The Bible encourages us to keep both a clean conscience and a pure heart. In Acts 24:16, Paul says, "I myself always strive to have a conscience without offense toward God and men." A clean conscience means we are free from the guilt of any known sin. A pure heart, however, goes even deeper. It's a heart focused on God alone, free from other distractions or attachments. Jesus told us, "Blessed are the pure in heart, for they shall see God" (Matthew 5:8). This means that those who stay focused on God, without being pulled away by other things, will be able to see God's work and presence in their lives.

A pure heart doesn't mean we are free from all sin or never experience a negative thought. The Apostle John reminds us, "If we say that we have no sin, we deceive ourselves" (1 John 1:8). This purity is not about being flawless but about having a heart that's sincere, undivided, and aligned with God's will.

In Scripture, the heart is not merely a metaphor for feelings but represents the very core of our being—our thoughts, desires, will, and spiritual inclinations. When Jesus speaks of being "pure in heart," He is calling us to a purity that reaches the deepest part of who we are, a purity of motives, desires, and actions. This purity is not attainable by outward acts alone but stems from a heart transformed by faith.

The apostle Peter underscores this in Acts 15:9, where he describes believers as having their hearts purified by faith. This shows that purity is a divine work within us, achieved by the grace of God through faith in Christ. We do not merely "try" to be pure; rather, we turn our hearts fully to Christ, allowing Him to cleanse and refine us.

The purification of our hearts is not a self-made achievement; it is a work of Christ that begins with faith. As Peter writes, "Since you have purified your souls in obeying the truth through the Spirit in sincere love of the brethren, love one another fervently with a pure heart" (1 Peter 1:22). Peter explains that through faith and obedience to the gospel, we receive a heart washed and prepared to love others sincerely. This transformation is not merely an outward change; it is a "heart transplant" accomplished by the Holy Spirit working in us.

The pure in heart shall see God. But

Impure Heart leads to Spiritual Blindness

Impure heart leads to spiritual blindness. Just like a drunk person can't see clearly, someone with an impure heart can't understand spiritual truths.

- A greedy person can't see the beauty of generosity. They are blinded by their desire for wealth and think being generous is foolish.
- An oppressive person can't see the wrong in their actions. They believe they are entitled to their position and that the suffering of others is justified.
- Someone living a morally corrupt life can't appreciate or understand the goodness of the gospel. Their impure actions prevent them from seeing spiritual truths.
- A double-minded person can't see God because they are not sincere. They are only interested in their own gain and can't understand true faith.

Jesus taught that an impure heart blinds us spiritually, distorting our perception of good and evil. Sin clouds our spiritual vision, much like intoxication clouds physical sight. For example, covetousness, a strong desire for wealth or possessions, blind us to the value of generosity. Proverbs 28:22 warns, "A man with an evil eye hastens after riches and does not consider that poverty will come upon him." Covetousness not only blinds us to the needs of others but distances us from God, who calls us to love and serve.

The Pure in Heart has a Single Focus

Jesus said, "Blessed are the pure in heart" (Matthew 5:8). This means blessed is the person whose heart is undivided, unmixed, and focused entirely on God. An undivided heart brings light and clarity to our lives. Matthew 6:22 says, "The eye is the lamp of the body; so then if your eye is clear, your whole body will be full of light."

Just as a healthy eye brings light to the body, a pure heart brings spiritual light and understanding. Danish theologian and philosopher Soren Kierkegaard explained, "Purity of heart is to will one thing." This means having a single-minded focus on God and His will.

Elijah challenged the people of Israel to stop wavering between God and idols. Similarly, we must choose between following Christ fully or being divided by worldly desires. James 4:8 tells us, "Purify your hearts, you double-minded," urging us to eliminate divided loyalties.

The Apostle Paul illustrates purity of heart in Philippians 3:13-14. He says, "Brethren, I do not count myself to have apprehended; but one thing I do, forgetting those things which are behind and reaching forward to those things which are ahead, I press toward the goal for the prize of the upward call of God in Christ Jesus."

Purity of heart is not perfection: "Not that I have already obtained this or am already perfect…"

Purity of heart is to will one thing: "One thing I do… I press on to take hold of the high calling for which Christ Jesus took hold of me."

- I will for it
- I try for it

- I press on toward it

When Jesus says, "Blessed are the pure in heart," he is saying, "Blessed is the person whose heart is undivided." Purity of heart means continually striving towards our calling in Christ - fully focused on the will of God - unmixed motive in serving God- free from the pollution of worldly desires or self-interest. In James 4:8, we're encouraged to "purify your hearts, you double-minded." This purity is about deciding fully for God rather than wavering between two loyalties. It's like Paul's one thing: "forgetting those things which are behind and reaching forward to those things which are ahead" (Philippians 3:13). David prayed in Psalm 51:10, "Create in me a clean heart, O God, and renew a steadfast spirit within me."

In Psalm 86:11, he prays, "Teach me Your way, O LORD; I will walk in Your truth; Unite my heart to fear Your name."

He is saying, "Lord, here's my heart, and it is all over the place, and I'm asking you to make it one, unite my heart, to make me a person who pursues only one thing- Fear your name that is to give reverence to your name.

This teaches us to pray for a united heart that seeks only God. Only His will. We should ask God to help us focus on Him and His truth.

An undivided - single, focused heart fully dedicated to God brings the blessing of seeing God more clearly and living in His light.

Jesus had a Single Focus- To do God's Will

Jesus demonstrated the ultimate example of an undivided heart by focusing only on doing the will of God during His time on Earth.

Jesus said, "My food is to do the will of him who sent me and to finish his work" (John 4:34). His main purpose and source of fulfilment were to obey God.

In the Garden of Gethsemane, Jesus prayed, "Not my will, but yours be done" (Luke 22:42). Even in moments of great distress, Jesus remained committed to God's plan.

When Jesus taught His followers to pray, "Your will be done, on earth as it is in heaven" (Matthew 6:10), He was speaking about the importance of aligning our desires with God's will.

Finally, Jesus said, "I have glorified You on the earth. I have finished the work which You have given Me to do." (John 17:4). His entire life was dedicated to completing God's mission, bringing glory to the Father through His actions.

By keeping a single focus on God's will, Jesus set the perfect example for us to follow.

The Blessing of a Pure Heart - Seeing God

Jesus tells us, "Blessed are the pure in heart, for they shall see God" (Matthew 5:8).

A pure heart finds God in the scripture. To some, the Scriptures might seem like a collection of ancient texts, but to those with a pure heart, every page, every chapter and every verse reveals God's character, His love, and His will.

Jesus promises that those who are pure in heart "shall see God." This is not a physical vision but a spiritual one, an insight into God's presence, God's character, and God's beauty. The apostle Paul elaborates on this in Ephesians 1:18, praying that the "eyes of [our] understanding" would be enlightened. It is through the eyes of our hearts that we "see" God, perceiving His presence in our lives, feeling His guidance, and understanding His ways.

Our vision of God becomes clearer and clearer as our heart grows purer and purer. Just as a mirror reflects an image more distinctly when it is free from blemishes, so does our heart reflect God's glory when it is cleansed of selfish motives, sinful thoughts, and worldly desires.

Imagine you're holding a white shirt. It looks perfectly clean in the dim light. You think, this shirt is spotless. But then, you step into a brighter light. Now, you notice a few faint stains that weren't visible before. You try to clean them off and think you're finished, but then you step into an even brighter light, and now you see even more marks and spots you couldn't see earlier.

In our journey of faith, Jesus calls us to "walk in the light." Walking in the light is the only way to become pure in heart. When we are in darkness or far from God, we might think we're clean and have nothing to worry about. But as we move closer to Him, His light will shine and reveal areas in our lives—sins, habits, thoughts—that we didn't notice before. The closer we get, the more we see. As we see these impurities, we can repent—turn away from them—and He helps us change.

Walking in God's light is a journey from darkness to glory and then to even more glory, as Paul says in 2 Corinthians 3:18. It's a process of God revealing more to us as we grow, transforming us to become more like Him. When we stay close to Jesus, He helps us see the stains, gently cleanses us, and brings us closer to a pure life that reflects His light fully.

As the psalmist says, "The Lord is near to all who call upon Him, to all who call upon Him in truth" (Psalm 145:18). This nearness is a result of living with a heart that earnestly seeks after God.

To see God, the heart must have a single focus, a perfect object that is pure in itself—Christ Jesus. He alone embodies the purity we seek, and by focusing on Him, we are transformed. The writer of Hebrews says, "Looking unto Jesus, the author and finisher of our faith" (Hebrews 12:2). As we look to Jesus, we not only see God revealed but also are transformed by what we see, becoming more and more like Him.

In our present state, we do not yet see God face-to-face, but through Christ, we glimpse His character and glory. First, John 3:2

gives a future promise: "Beloved, now we are children of God; and it has not yet been revealed what we shall be, but we know that when He is revealed, we shall be like Him, for we shall see Him as He is." The final vision of God awaits, but even now, in faith, we experience the joy and satisfaction of seeing God's goodness and beauty.

A pure heart begins to grasp the depth of God's character—His love, justice, mercy, power, and grace. This understanding is more than merely seeing His works; it's about knowing who God is.

Those with a pure heart experience a close, personal relationship with God.

- They feel His presence,
- hear His guidance, and
- find comfort in His love.

The bond of a living union in which Christ becomes yours, and you become his. You are "in Christ," and Christ is in you.

Ultimately, those who are pure in heart will see God in heaven.

In summary, a pure heart opens the way to

- a deeper understanding of God's character,
- a closer relationship with Him, and
- the hope of an eternal future in His presence.

The greatest reward of purity is the vision of God Himself. As Revelation 22:4 promises, "They shall see His face, and His name shall be on their foreheads." This vision is the consummation of all we long for in our faith journey—the moment when we shall know Him fully, just as we are fully known.

Pure in Heart means having a single focused heart with an unmixed motive. "Blessed are the pure in heart, for they shall see God." Matt 5:8.

Blessed are the Peacemakers, For they
shall be called sons of God.

Chapter 7

"Blessed are the Peacemakers, For they shall be called sons of God." (Matthew 5:9)

In the Bible, the number seven often represents completeness or perfection, and it seems fitting that Jesus placed the peacemaker here, as if showing that this is a key part of what it means to be a true Christian. The Beatitudes give us a clear picture of what a Christian's character should look like, with each step leading us closer to God's heart. And now, we arrive at this crucial character: "Blessed are the peacemakers."

This role is significant. We need to be "pure first, then peaceable" because genuine peace doesn't mean giving up doing the right thing. To be a peacemaker, you have to stand firm in what is right while working for peace.

The Bible speaks about "violence and strife in the city" (Psalm 55:9).

In our own city, we see conflict and violence, not just from outside but from within our families, communities, and even our own hearts. There is violence in the city because there is violence in the family, and there is violence in the family because there is violence in our hearts. A pure heart is inevitable to be a peacemaker.

When David says, "I see violence and strife in the city," he is talking about the city of God. The strife and violence did not come from invading armies. It rose up from among the people of God themselves. Across the globe, regardless of culture or belief, people yearn for peace. In war-torn regions, fractured families, and contentious relationships, the desire for peace is universal.

In Genesis 6:11, it states, "The earth was filled with violence." God, witnessing the rampant evil, sent a flood to cleanse the earth, saving only Noah and his family, who found grace in His eyes. This cycle of violence persists throughout scripture, as seen in David's lament in Psalm 55, where he speaks of violence and strife in the city. The prophet Ezekiel also lamented, saying, "The land is full of bloody crimes" (Ezekiel 7:23).

Albert Einstein, who was awarded the Nobel Prize in Physics in 1921, addressed the looming danger of nuclear warfare in a 1948 lecture. He commented on the threat of nuclear warfare. He said, "The true issue is not physical, but ethical. It is not the sheer force of the atomic bomb that frightens us, but the explosive potential of human wickedness—the capacity of the human heart for boundless evil."

The heart of the issue lies within us. James 4:1-2 poses a critical question: "Where do wars and fights come from among you? Do they not come from your desires for pleasure that war in your members?" The conflict we experience externally mirrors the battles within our hearts. Our desires—selfish, greedy, and often destructive—fuel the strife around us.

As mentioned in the previous chapters, Beatitudes build on one another, creating a spiritual ladder. Those who are pure in heart (Matthew 5:8) are naturally inclined to seek peace, yet genuine peacemaking is not a natural human instinct. In a world driven by conflict and strife, the call to be a peacemaker is both counter-cultural and challenging. Here, the message is very clear: If we are not merciful, we face judgment. Without purity, we cannot see God. If we are not peacemakers, we are left outside God's family. These descriptions point to our final salvation, promised only to those who accept these transformative virtues. The Beatitudes, therefore, directly confront any notion that mere belief, without change, secures eternal life. Beatitudes are not an optional suggestion of Jesus for His followers, but it's a call to non-negotiable Christian walk.

When we explore what it means to be a peacemaker, let's remember that it's not just about avoiding conflict. It's about actively seeking to make things right, rooted in a pure heart that comes from knowing Jesus. It's a tough task, but it reflects God's own heart for us.

What It Means to Be a Peacemaker

The Character of a Peacemaker

The peacemaker chooses to act differently even though they live in the same world as everyone else and face the same problems and temptations.

A peacemaker's actions are rooted in an inner peace that comes from a pure heart—a heart that is single-minded in its devotion to God and His will. This purity is essential because it aligns the peacemaker's desires and actions with God's purposes.

As Jesus taught, "Blessed are the pure in heart, for they shall see God" (Matthew 5:8), and immediately following, "Blessed are the peacemakers, for they shall be called sons of God" (Matthew 5:9). The connection between these two beatitudes is crucial: purity comes before peace. True peace cannot come from a divided heart, one that is split between opposing desires or loyalties.

As James writes, "The wisdom from above is first pure, then peaceable" (James 3:17).

The peacemaker, therefore, actively pursues purity—striving to align every aspect of their life with God's will. They understand that unsettled conflict in their own hearts will eventually flow over into their relationships, bringing disharmony.

The heart of the issue lies within us. James 4:1-2 poses a critical question: "Where do wars and fights come from among you? Do they not come from your desires for pleasure that war in your members?" The conflict we experience externally mirrors the battles within our hearts. Our desires—selfish, greedy, and often destructive—fuel the strife around us.

For the peacemaker, this inner peace is not just a personal comfort; it is a gift they are called to share with others. They bring peace into their homes, workplaces, and communities because they themselves are at peace. They do not shy away from conflict but engage with it from a place of stability and calm, aiming to bring resolution and reconciliation wherever they go. Their actions are guided by the principle that peace is not merely the absence of conflict but the presence of righteousness and justice.

In this way, the peacemaker becomes a true reflection of God's character, representing His love and mercy in a world that is often broken by division and conflict.

Peacemakers are people who bring peace to others because they have peace within themselves.

How Do You Get Peace?

Peace in your heart comes from purity in your life. Notice the order in the Beatitudes: "Blessed are the pure in heart, for they shall see God." (Matthew 5:8) And then, "Blessed are the peacemakers, for they shall be called sons of God." (Matthew 5:9) There's a direct connection here.

"The wisdom from above is first pure, then peaceable." Purity comes first, then peace. Peace of heart flows from the purity of life. Why? Because purity of heart means wanting one thing above all else. A person who desires one thing wholeheartedly can be at peace. But an impure person has a heart that is divided—they want two contradictory things at the same time. As long as that inner conflict burns, there can be no peace.

James addresses this when he asks, "What causes quarrels and fights among you? Is it not this, that your passions are at war within you?" (James 4:1-2) When our desires are at war within us, we are torn in different directions, unable to find peace. Without purity, peace is impossible.

God has called us to peace

There are two kinds of people: peacemakers and peace breakers. God calls us to be peacemakers in a world full of conflict.

1 Corinthians 7:15 says that 'God has called us to peace.' If you belong to Jesus, this is your calling. God wants you to contribute to the peace of your family—whether it's your parents, siblings, or children. No matter if your family is close-knit or struggling with tension, God calls you to do your best to bring peace. Whether your family is functional or dysfunctional, you are called to be an influence for good, helping to make things better.

The same applies to the church. As a member of the congregation, you are called to contribute to its peace. This is not just a suggestion; it's a calling from God. The same goes for your workplace, your community, or even when you're out in public.

Wherever you are, whatever you do, God has called you to peace.

Plan for Peace

In Proverbs 12:20, the Bible says, "Those who plan peace have joy." (Proverbs 12:20)

Since God calls us to peace, we should be intentional about pursuing it. We should plan for peace!

Where we don't have peace, we should ask ourselves, "What's the best way to achieve it?" And where we do have peace, we should ask, "How can we protect it? How do we ensure we don't lose it?"

In the Bible, peace, or "shalom," is more than just the absence of conflict. It's the active enjoyment of all that is good. As we think about what we say and do, we should ask ourselves, "What would promote peace?" What would bring the greatest health and peace to

- our family,
- our church,
- our colleagues
- our neighbors
- our friends and
- our community?

We should plan for that—plot it, strategize for it. Because those who plan peace experience great joy!

Work for Peace

The Bible tells us, "Strive for peace with everyone, and for the holiness without which no one will see the Lord." (Hebrews 12:14)

Romans 14:19 says "Let us therefore make every effort to do what leads to peace and to mutual edification."

Peacemakers don't stop with just planning; they work out their plans. The word "strive" suggests effort, hard work, and persistence. There's a reason why being a peacemaker is the seventh beatitude—it's the peak, the summit of Christian character.

Why Peacemakers are Called Sons of God

"Blessed are the peacemakers, for they shall be called sons of God." — Matthew 5:9

When Jesus says that peacemakers will be called "sons of God," He is telling us something important about who they are. This title shows that peacemakers share in the character of God and are connected to Him in a special way.

God: The Source of All Peace

In the Bible, God is called "the God of peace" (Hebrews 13:20; 1 Thessalonians 5:23; Romans 15:33). This means that God is the one who creates and gives peace. Within Himself, God exists in perfect harmony, especially in the relationship between the Father, the Son, and the Holy Spirit. There is no conflict or disagreement among them—only perfect unity and love. This shows that peace is a part of who God is.

Jesus is also known as the "Prince of Peace" (Isaiah 9:6). He came to establish peace between God and humanity. When Jesus was born, angels announced, "Glory to God in the highest, and on earth peace among those with whom he is pleased!" (Luke 2:14).

The Holy Spirit is also called the "Spirit of Peace" (Matthew 3:16).

Peacemakers Reflect God's Peace

When Jesus calls peacemakers "sons of God," He is saying that they show what God is like. Being a peacemaker means working to bring people together, just like God brings us close to Him. It's about helping others find peace with God and with each other.

Peacemakers are recognized as "sons of God" because their lives mirror the peace-making mission of Christ, who came to reconcile humanity to God and to one another.

Just like children often look like their parents, peacemakers resemble God. Their actions reveal God's love and peace to the world. When we work to make peace, we show others who God is and what He does.

God's Way of Making Peace

God's example of making peace teaches us how we should do it. It involves humility, sacrifice, and loving others—even when it's difficult.

Don't Stand on Your Rights

Jesus, even though He was God, didn't hold onto His rights.

- He humbled Himself
- He gave up all His rights,

- He became human, and
- He died on the cross
- to make peace between us and God (Philippians 2:5-8).

In the same way, we are called to let go of our rights sometimes, for the sake of making peace.

If Jesus had insisted on His rights, we would still be separated from God. We would still be consigned for hell.

Making peace often means putting others first, even when it's hard. As Paul says, "… with humility consider one another as more important than yourselves; 4do not merely look out for your own personal interests, but also for the interests of others." (Phil 2:3-4)

Every time you think about your rights, remind yourself, "If Jesus stood on his rights, I would be in hell forever, and so would everyone else."

You cannot make peace by standing on your rights.

Love First; before being loved in return

God's love is given freely, even when it's not returned. Romans 5:8 says, "God demonstrates his own love for us in this: While we were still sinners, Christ died for us."

God's love is not based on what we do but on His own goodness. As peacemakers, we are called to love others in the same way, even if they don't love us back. This kind of love comes from the Holy Spirit, who helps us love like Jesus.

In simple terms, peacemakers are called "sons of God" because they show the world what God is like. They bring peace, just as God brings peace, and through their actions, they reveal His love and goodness to others.

Our Limitations

Most of us can think of a relationship that didn't end the way we wanted it to. Sometimes, despite our best efforts, we may not be able to make peace. We live in a fallen world, and even at our best, we are sinners in need of grace. Others are also in the same situation.

We may feel like David in Psalm 55, weeping in the hurt of betrayal by those close to him.... struggling with the pain of broken relationships. How do we live with that?

There's only one answer to that: "Cast your burden upon the Lord, and he will sustain you. He will never permit the righteous to be moved" (Psalm 55:22).

Chronicles chapter 20, verse 12 says. "O our God, will You not judge them? That is, will you not solve this? For we have no power against this great multitude that is coming against us; nor do we know what to do, but our eyes *are* upon You."

That is

- We have no power

- We have no Wisdom and
- We trust in you

And the Lord answered their prayer in verse 17. He said, "You will not *need* to fight in this *battle*. Position yourselves, stand still and see the salvation of the Lord, who is with you.."

Continue to trust in God, who calls us to peace and promises to sustain us.

Blessed are those who are persecuted for righteousness' sake, For theirs is the kingdom of heaven.

Chapter 8

**"Blessed are those who are persecuted for righteousness'
sake, For theirs is the kingdom of heaven." (Matthew 5:10)**

Each Beatitude is a stepping stone, revealing a deeper dimension
of our call to be set apart, to reflect Christ's character, and to walk in
His ways. Through each blessing, Jesus has not only revealed the
heart of God but has also provided a blueprint for a life that is
transformed by His Spirit.

To be poor in spirit is to recognize our utter nothingness apart
from God, to acknowledge our complete dependence upon Him, and
to humbly seek His grace and mercy (Matthew 5:3). To mourn over
our sins is to go beyond mere recognition of our need; it is to feel the
weight of our sins, understanding the cost, and seeking true
repentance that transforms the heart (Matthew 5:4). To walk in
meekness is to surrender fully to the will of God, allowing His Spirit
to shape us from our natural, wild state into Christlikeness (Matthew
5:5). These three attitudes form the root of Christian life, for without
them, there is no genuine Christianity. From these roots, however, a
godly life springs forth and matures a life that hungers and thirsts for
righteousness, passionately desiring the presence and righteousness
of God to guide every decision and action (Matthew 5:6).

When cultivated, this life bears the fruits of mercy—being
compassionate toward others, forgiving wrongs, and extending
ourselves to those in need (Matthew 5:7). It grows into purity of heart,

a singular devotion to God, purging the double-mindedness that competes with our love for Christ (Matthew 5:8). Finally, it blossoms into a peacemaking spirit, reflecting Christ's peace-giving mission, manifesting God's love and peace within a divided world (Matthew 5:9). This is the path of sanctification, the life to which God calls us, and the life where His divine blessing abides.

But what can we expect if we pursue such a life?

Jesus gives us two answers:

- You will be persecuted by the world, and
- You will be blessed by God.

Ultimately, the Beatitudes reveal a sobering truth: following Jesus comes with sacrifice. "Blessed are those who are persecuted for righteousness' sake, For theirs is the kingdom of heaven. Blessed are you when they revile and persecute you and say all kinds of evil against you falsely for My sake". — Matthew 5:10-11. This final Beatitude highlights the reality of persecution for those who follow Christ with sincerity and encapsulates the inevitable cost of discipleship in a world often hostile to God's values. Yet, this very suffering brings with it a promise of joy and eternal communion with God, known in Scripture as the true meaning of blessedness (1 Timothy 1:11, 6:15; Titus 2:13).

Persecution for Righteousness' Sake

At the heart of these verses is the idea that living a life of righteousness — one that aligns with God's will and reflects His character—will naturally lead to opposition. The suffering that Jesus describes here is not merely the everyday hardships we experience due to the fallen nature of the world (Romans 8:18–25). It is not the result of personal faults like judgmentalism, hypocrisy, or simply being difficult to get along with. Nor is it the kind of imagined persecution that arises from self-centered sensitivity or political identity. Rather, this blessing is reserved for those who endure suffering because of their commitment to righteousness—that is, those who suffer for faithfully obeying God's will.

In John 15:18-20, Jesus reminds us that if the world hated Him, it would hate His followers as well. Persecution for righteousness' sake happens because the values of God's kingdom sharply contrast with the ways of the world (Isaiah 55:9). Following Jesus with a steadfast heart will invite opposition, whether through social rejection, exclusion, or, in more extreme cases, imprisonment and even death.

"Blessed are you when people insult you, persecute you, and falsely say all kinds of evil against you because of me." This is not persecution for personal reasons or because of something wrong we've done, but for His sake—because of our identification with Christ. This connects with 1 Peter 4:14: "If you are insulted because of the name of Christ, you are blessed, for the Spirit of glory and of God rests on you."

Why are we Persecuted?

We are not of this World

"Persecution comes only to those who are committed to God's standards of righteousness—those who are truly following Jesus and have chosen not to compromise with the world—not simply to those who suffer for any reason. "Jesus said, "If you were of the world, the world would love its own. But because you are not of the world... the world hates you" (John 15:19). Christians do not belong to this world, and the world hates that.

Paul writes in 2 Timothy 3:12, "All who desire to live godly in Christ Jesus will suffer persecution." Those who are committed to living for Christ will inevitably face opposition. If we're not experiencing any pushback for our faith, it may be because we're blending in too much with the world. Jesus warns us to be careful when the world only speaks well of us (Luke 6:26). If we never face any challenge or opposition, we might need to examine if we're truly living boldly for Him.

Why is this the case? The message of Christianity often runs counter to worldly beliefs and desires. Those who seek purity, humility, and self-control can seem like a reproach to others. This creates a natural tension between believers and the world. As Christians pursue righteousness, their lives can expose worldly pursuits challenging values like pride, materialism, and indulgence.

They do not know God

Jesus also warned that persecution comes because people do not know the Father or the Son. "They will ban you from the synagogue, yet an hour is coming for everyone who kills you to think that he is offering a service to God. These things they will do because they have not known the Father nor Me." (John 16:2-3). In ignorance, they oppose the truth and even believe they are doing God's work by persecuting the righteous.

They Love Darkness

The root cause of persecution lies in a conflict between godly living and self-justification. When believers live with purity, humility, and love, it can bring to light the selfish or impure motives of others. In John 3:20-21, we see two responses to this kind of godly living: "Everyone who does evil hates the light and does not come to the light, lest his deeds should be exposed." This hatred for the light is a root cause of persecution.

Opposition is a Normal Christian Experience

So, the righteousness that we pursue as Christians is in conflict with the world's values. When we stand for truth, justice, and godly principles, we will face resistance, criticism, or even persecution.

The Apostle Paul reinforces this in 2 Timothy 3:12: He says

"Indeed, all who want to live in a godly way in Christ Jesus will be persecuted."

That is everyone...not some or not most .... but all who want to live a godly life in Christ Jesus will be persecuted.

I 100% believe that the Bible is totally inspired by God, and Paul says all who desire or all who want to live a godly life will be persecuted. Jesus said in John 15:20, 'If they persecuted me, they will also persecute you." That is again a 'WILL' there. They will persecute you. He said in John 15:20, "A servant is not greater than his master. If they persecuted me, they will also persecute you. Opposition is not exceptional but normal for Christians. Look at the lives of people throughout the Bible.

Here is the one Who endured the greatest persecution - His name is Jesus - Isaiah 53:3-4 reveals the depths of His suffering: "He was despised and rejected by men, a man of sorrows and acquainted with grief." He faced scorn from His own brothers (John 7:5), threats from those who sought His life (John 5:18), betrayal from a disciple (Luke 22:48), and abandonment by His followers (Matthew 26:56). He was mocked and abused by Roman soldiers (Matthew 27:27-31) and crucified alongside criminals (Matthew 27:38), enduring a death He did not deserve.

Jesus did not merely endure this persecution; He did so willingly, knowing full well what lay ahead. His capacity to face such agony was rooted in the joy that would come from His sacrifice. "Looking to Jesus, the founder and perfecter of our faith, who for the joy that was set before Him endured the cross..." (Hebrews 12:2).

Persecution for righteousness' sake began in the very first family. Adam and Eve had two sons, Cain and Abel. Cain killed his brother, not because of a mere quarrel, but because "his own deeds were evil and his brother's righteous" (1 John 3:12). Abel was the first martyr, setting the pattern for those who would follow in suffering for righteousness' sake.

- Consider Joseph, who was persecuted by his brothers and imprisoned in Egypt for his faithfulness (Genesis 37, 39).
- Moses was reviled and rejected by the Israelites (Exodus 5:21; 14:11), and
- Samuel was rejected (1 Samuel 8:5).
- Elijah faced persecution from King Ahab and Jezebel (1 Kings 18:17; 19:2), and
- Nehemiah was oppressed and de-famed (Nehemiah 4).

In the New Testament,

- Stephen was stoned
- Peter and John were imprisoned, and
- James was beheaded.
- Apostle Paul's entire Christian life was marked by persecution.

The pattern continues throughout the early church.

The Philippians were told that it had been "granted" to them to suffer for Christ's sake: For it has been granted to you that for the sake of Christ, you should not only believe in him but also suffer for his sake. (Philippians 1:29)

The Thessalonians were commended for enduring persecution and affliction with steadfastness: "We ourselves boast about you in the churches of God for your steadfastness and faith in all your persecutions and in the afflictions that you are enduring. (2 Thessalonians 1:4)

"In Pontus, Galatia, Cappadocia, Asia, and Bithynia: do not be surprised by the fiery trial that comes to test you, as though something unusual were happening to you." (1 Peter 4:12)

Suffering from being a Christian is normal because the sinful nature is hostile to God (Romans 8:7).

Jesus Himself, who lived out each one of these Beatitudes, was persecuted.

Forms of Persecution

Jesus said in Matthew 5:11, "Blessed are you when others revile you and persecute you and utter all kinds of evil against you falsely on my account." He identifies three forms of opposition: verbal abuse, physical persecution, and false accusations. Christian persecution can come in any of these forms, ranging from insults and mockery to physical violence, imprisonment, or even death.

Luke's account of this reads, "Blessed are you when people hate you and when they exclude you and revile you and spurn your name as evil, on account of the Son of Man." Luke 6:22-23

Persecution isn't just about physical harm; it includes emotional and social rejection, exclusion, and hatred. We see this kind of reviling in how people mocked Jesus during His trial and crucifixion, slandering His identity and message. Likewise, Christians today face verbal persecution in many forms—whether through bullying at school, discrimination in the workplace, or media portrayals that mock our faith.

Throughout the church's history, genuine Christians have faced high levels of persecution and discrimination. This persecution ranges from verbal abuse to imprisonment and martyrdom, all because of their commitment to Christ. Whether mild or severe, every Christian should expect some form of opposition to their faith. But Jesus calls us to "rejoice and be glad" because our reward in heaven is great, and we stand in the company of the prophets who endured the same (Matthew 5:12).

This eighth Beatitude sets the expectation for a normal Christian life: those who follow Christ will be blessed by God and persecuted by the world.

The Father's Discipline and Love

- Have you ever experienced any persecution in your life?
- Have you ever been rebuked or disciplined by God?

Bible says,

"For the Lord disciplines the one he loves and chastises every son whom he receives." Hebrews 12:6

"Those whom I love I rebuke and discipline." Revelation 3:19

Persecution is not only an inevitable part of living a godly life, but it is also an opportunity for spiritual growth.

When we experience opposition or hardship for our faith, it can serve as a refining process. God allows hardships to

- shape our character,
- deepen our dependence on Him, and
- draw us closer to Him.

Romans 5:3-5 tells us that suffering produces perseverance, character, and hope. In enduring persecution, we not only share in Christ's sufferings (Philippians 3:10), but we also experience the power of His resurrection and His sustaining grace.

Persevering Through Opposition

Persecution often brings the temptation to take the easy way out. In a culture that offers endless choices, we can fall into the habit of avoiding difficulty. But perseverance is key to spiritual growth. James reminds us in James 1:2-4 that trials produce perseverance, which leads to maturity in our faith.

There is a time for standing firm and a time for moving on. But we should resist the impulse to always choose what's easiest. Hebrews 12:6 tells us that God disciplines those He loves, using hardship to refine us. Moving from job to job, church to church, or place to place when things get tough may bring short-term relief, but it also prevents us from growing deeper in faith.

What if we aren't experiencing persecution?

One thing to examine is whether our lives are truly reflecting the righteousness of Christ.

Do I really belong to that category of people mentioned in those words, those who desire to live godly in Christ Jesus?

If so, I will be persecuted. If I'm not persecuted scripture is having to pass away. This word will not pass away. Then … whatever I may think about myself, I'm not really seeking to live godly in Christ. I'm probably a compromiser, a chameleon that changes colour according to society.

Christian chameleons will not be persecuted when they're in the midst of holy people. They use religious language. When they're in the midst of unconverted friends and relatives, they gossip and backbite just like anybody else. Such people will never be persecuted because such people are chameleons who change their colour according to the group they are with.

A chameleon is not a child of God. A cat cannot change its nature when it's among the pigs and, you know, be dirty like the pig. A cat is a cat wherever it goes. In the same way, if you're really born from above, and God is putting in you a desire by his spirit to live godly, you will be persecuted.

When we talk about persecution, I'm not necessarily talking about being thrown to the lions being burned or beheaded, but some form of persecution. As we said, it may be mental, verbal…emotional.

We had a friend who was working as a manager of a bank in India. In her line of work, she was facing pressure to manipulate financial records, lie to customers, etc —things that go against a godly conscience. She refused to compromise and ended up losing her job because of that.

It's easy to avoid persecution by blending in with the world. But that's not what Jesus calls us to. He calls us to shine as light. Living as true Christians may bring trouble, But Jesus reassures us that we are blessed because such experiences confirm that we belong to Him.

Should we Flee Persecution?

Is it ever right to escape persecution? This is a practical question for many Christians. Should we encourage our children to leave a school where they face opposition for their faith? Should we quit a job where it's hard to be a Christian? John Bunyan, who was imprisoned for 12 years in England for preaching, offers wise counsel.

He reminds us that Jesus said to be "wise as serpents and innocent as doves" (Matthew 10:16).

There are times when it is right to flee. Jesus told His disciples, "If they persecute you in one city, flee to another" (Matthew 10:23). The same person may flee at one time and stand firm at another, depending on God's leading.

- Moses fled when Pharaoh sought to kill him (Exodus 2:15);
- Moses stood (Hebrews 11:27) and left Egypt, without fearing Pharaoh's wrath.
- David fled (1 Samuel 19:12) when Saul tried to kill him
- David stood (1 Samuel 24:8) confronting Saul, showing mercy and trusting God to judge.
- Jeremiah fled (Jeremiah 37:11-12): trying to leave Jerusalem
- Jeremiah stood (Jeremiah 38:17): before King Zedekiah, delivering God's message to surrender.
- Christ withdrew Himself (Luke 9:10): following the assassination of John the Baptist.
- Christ (John 18:1-8): willingly stood before His captors in the Garden of Gethsemane.
- Paul fled (2 Corinthians 11:33): Damascus by being lowered in a basket through the city wall.
- Paul stood (Acts 20:22-23): firm, ready to face suffering in Jerusalem for the sake of the gospel.

Bunyan advises that if God directs you to stand, stand. If God directs you to fly, fly. The key is to follow God's will. There are no rigid rules, but rather the guidance of the Holy Spirit. The decision to stay or flee should be made with a heart that seeks to honor God above all else without denying the truth.

The Kingdom of Heaven Is Ours

Jesus closes the Beatitude in Matthew 5:10-11 with the promise that those who are persecuted for righteousness' sake will inherit the Kingdom of Heaven. This echoes Matthew 5:3, where the "poor in spirit" are also promised the Kingdom. To endure persecution for the sake of Christ is to live as heirs of His Kingdom—a Kingdom that is eternal and unshakable.

Paul's words in Romans 8:18 provide further comfort:

"I consider that our present sufferings are not worth comparing with the glory that will be revealed in us."

Whatever we face in this life—no matter how difficult—cannot compare to the eternal glory we will experience with Christ. This is the ultimate hope that sustains us through persecution: knowing that we are part of an everlasting Kingdom, and the suffering of this world is temporary.

Conclusion

Persecution is not something we seek, but it is something we are called to endure for the sake of Christ. Paul said, "For I consider that the sufferings of this present time are not worth comparing with the glory that is to be revealed to us." (Romans 8:18). Our suffering is not in vain; it is part of a glorious promise that binds us to Christ and to one another in faith.

As followers of Jesus, we will face challenges, opposition, and even suffering because we stand for righteousness. But in the midst of this, we are blessed—blessed with the assurance of God's presence, the promise of His Kingdom, and the deep joy that comes from walking faithfully with Him.

Conclusion

As we reach the conclusion of this journey through the Beatitudes, we come face-to-face with the transformative power of Jesus' words and His call to a life that both transcends and confronts the world. Each Beatitude has revealed not only a blessing but a way of being— a progressive path of spiritual transformation, unveiling God's heart for His people and the character He seeks in us as kingdom citizens.

In these verses, Jesus has given us more than a list of good values; He has shown us a roadmap for living in close communion with God and in alignment with His kingdom values. The Beatitudes illuminate a life where humility, mercy, purity, and peace are not abstract ideals but living realities. In this life, God's blessings flow, and His presence is felt deeply, marking us as His own. This life calls us to look beyond ourselves, to hunger and thirst for righteousness, to show mercy as we have received mercy, and to be peacemakers in a divided world.

Adopting our Identity as the Blessed of God

To live by the Beatitudes is to live with a clear understanding of our identity and purpose in Christ. Jesus declares that we are blessed—not in the temporary, conditional sense that the world often suggests, but in the enduring, eternal sense that aligns with the heart of God. To be blessed in this way is to be favored by God, to find our true home in His kingdom, and to know that our lives have purpose and meaning beyond earthly circumstances.

As we conclude this study on the Beatitudes, we stand in awe of Jesus' call to a life that is marked not only by spiritual growth but also by the experience of great blessing. Each Beatitude has unfolded a way of being that is rewarded with a unique form of divine favor—a blessedness that brings the lasting joy that every heart seeks. This joy is a foretaste of God's kingdom, offering a deep, abiding satisfaction that transcends worldly pleasure.

In living out these truths daily, we're not just following Jesus' teachings; we're living a life that visibly reflects His kingdom here on earth. The Beatitudes offer us both the promise of blessedness and the privilege of transformation. As each Beatitude works within us, may we find joy not only in our growth but in the unshakable assurance that we are blessed—deeply and eternally—by the One who called us to this path.

When we recognize this blessing, our perspective shifts. We begin to see trials and challenges not as barriers but as opportunities for spiritual growth. We see persecution, rejection, and sacrifice as invitations to share in Christ's sufferings, drawing us nearer to Him and strengthening our commitment to live for His glory. Our lives are no longer governed by the fleeting pleasures or fears of this world; instead, we find peace, joy, and hope in the pursuit of righteousness and in the presence of our Savior.

Becoming Salt and Light in a Dark World

The Beatitudes culminate in the call to be "salt" and "light" in the world (Matthew 5:13-16). Just as salt preserves and flavors, our lives are meant to preserve what is good, adding depth and meaning to the lives of those around us. Light, on the other hand, dispels darkness and illuminates the truth. In a world that often feels cold and shadowed by despair, we are called to radiate Christ's love, offering hope and pointing others to the Light of the World.

Living as salt and light means more than simply professing faith; it involves living out the Beatitudes in every area of our lives. Our interactions, decisions, and relationships should reflect the values of God's kingdom. When we live in this way, our lives become testimonies to the transformative power of God's grace, drawing others toward the truth of His love.

The Cost and Reward of Following Christ

As we commit to walking in the way of the Beatitudes, we must also count the cost. Jesus has warned that a life aligned with God's values may attract opposition and persecution. Yet, He has assured us that such suffering is temporary and that the reward is eternal. Every sacrifice we make, every rejection we endure, and every hardship we face for His sake draws us closer to the kingdom of heaven. It is a reminder that our ultimate home is not here but with our Father.

In the face of opposition, we can take comfort in knowing that Jesus walked this path before us. He faced rejection, persecution, and even death, but He triumphed over all through His resurrection. His victory assures us that we, too, will share in His triumph. The trials we endure for righteousness' sake are not without purpose; they mold us into His likeness, fortify our faith, and deepen our joy in His presence.

Ever growing, Ever becoming

As we reach the end of this study, we're reminded that the Beatitudes outline a lifelong journey—a continual process of growing closer to Christ as each beatitude matures alongside the others. Each Beatitude forms an essential part of our spiritual transformation. While they progress in a meaningful sequence—beginning with poverty of spirit and culminating in the courage to endure persecution—no single Beatitude is ever "complete." Instead, they unfold, each supporting the growth of the others. For instance, being "poor in spirit" grounds us in humility, enabling us to develop meekness and hunger for righteousness. But as we grow in these areas, our need for spiritual poverty deepens, and we find ourselves revisiting and reexamining these truths.

As we live in this way, we aren't simply following Jesus' teachings; we're becoming a visible testimony of His kingdom here on earth. And while we never fully "arrive" at any one Beatitude, we are constantly being transformed—step by step, thread by thread, flow by flow—into His image. This journey will continue until we stand fully redeemed before Him, knowing that each step, however small, draws us closer to our Savior's likeness. "Beloved, now we are children of God, and it has not yet been revealed what we shall be, but we know that when He is revealed, we shall be like Him, for we shall see Him as He is." (1 John 3:2)

A Call to Live the Beatitudes Daily

As we close, the challenge remains: to live the Beatitudes not just in moments of inspiration but in the ordinary rhythms of daily life. The Beatitudes are not a checklist to complete; they are an invitation to a lifelong journey of faith, surrender, and transformation. Each Beatitude calls us to adopt a kingdom perspective that shapes our values, choices, and actions.

May we live with a spirit of humility, always aware of our need for God. May we mourn over sin and seek true repentance, allowing His grace to heal and transform us. May we hunger and thirst for righteousness, pursue peace, and extend mercy to others as we have been shown mercy. And may we, even in times of persecution, rejoice in the assurance that we belong to Christ and that ours is the kingdom of heaven.

As we step forward, may our lives reflect the beauty of the Beatitudes, bearing witness to the power of God's kingdom here and now. Let us hold to this high calling, confident that He who began this work in us will be faithful to complete it. With grateful hearts and steadfast spirits, let us live as kingdom citizens, manifesting the beatitudes and carrying His light into the world.

---

www.ingramcontent.com/pod-product-compliance
Lightning Source LLC
Chambersburg PA
CBHW031624040426

42452CB00007B/661